Proper Stations

Also by Richard Faber

*

THE VISION AND THE NEED
BEACONSFIELD AND BOLINGBROKE

Proper Stations

Class in Victorian Fiction

RICHARD FABER

FABER AND FABER

3 Queen Square

London

First published in 1971
by Faber and Faber Limited
3 Queen Square London WC1
Printed in Great Britain by
W & J Mackay Ltd, Chatham
All rights reserved

ISBN 0 571 09566 6

© Richard Faber 1971

Contents

*   *   *

The drawing reproduced on the title-page is one
of Thackeray's own illustrations for *The Book of
Snobs*.

'O let us love our occupations,
Bless the squire and his relations,
Live upon our daily rations,
And always know our proper stations.'

(As set to music by Lady Bowley for the men and boys in the village in Dickens's *The Chimes*.)

1. Introduction

The rich man in his castle,
The poor man at his gate:
God made them, high or lowly,
And order'd their estate.

Most Victorians took their 'estate' for granted. They lived at a time of great material progress, much new wealth, intense intellectual activity and steady political reform. But their social and moral assumptions often seem those of a static society: this gives an illusion of stillness to a period that was full of movement.

The stillness is not all illusory. There was a good deal of climbing up and down the ladder; but the ladder itself stood still. Even in times of distress, responsible and established people were slow to question a social structure which had enabled the country to become rich and powerful—and which still allowed room for growth. It was only natural that the orthodox should regard its sanction as divine. More complex, more class-conscious, but scarcely less hierarchical than in the previous century, the system had developed a classic assurance, an Augustan bloom. Its stability was the trellis on which doubt, reform and enterprise flourished. It offered the enterprising and successful a sense of purpose and achievement; the reformers, both a base and a target; the thinkers, space and shelter. It was oppressive, but not to the point of crushing vigour or the forces that were eventually to transform it.

The canons of Victorian society, though they once seemed so unalterable, no longer—or only dimly—prevail. They had their silver age in the first half of this century and they are not yet irrelevant. But so much in our social attitudes is changing that we may soon need a real effort of imagination to think ourselves back in that once familiar mould. It is not too early (it might soon be getting late) for the tranquil recollection of Victorian snobbery.

This book relies solely on fiction, in order to limit what would otherwise be a vast field for research. Parts of that wider field have of course already been worked by better qualified historians. But any social structure is so much a matter of sentiment and prejudice

that the descriptions given by contemporary novelists may be as worth studying from one point of view as statistics are from another. Novels begin by reflecting the structure, and end by confirming, or modifying it. Our own ideas of our dissolving and re-forming society are affected by novels and films, which help to set or change the tone as well as capture it. Victorian novelists worked within a more established social framework. Hence they had less scope for evaluating social importance differently and their accounts, however slanted, tally closer than those of modern novelists are likely to do a century from now. Some of the Victorian novelists were more at home with certain segments of society than with others; their personal reactions to the system differed; but the social world in which their creatures moved is real, solid and, essentially, one. The classic age of English society—as it seems in retrospect—was also the classic age of English fiction. Except for a few uncharted areas, the novelists knew where they stood (whether or not they liked it) and so did their readers.

My period is the half century from, roughly, 1830 to 1880. This excludes the later Victorian novelists with their more private, or at least more highly contrasting, pictures of society. It also allows some unity of theme. During these decades the aristocracy and landed gentry, although less powerful than they had been, were still predominant in government and the countryside. Their social prestige, which had substantially survived the changes of the thirties and forties, was to weaken under agricultural depression, electoral and military reform, the opening of the civil service to competitive examination and the growing power of finance on the one hand and organized labour on the other. But this decline did not really set in until the closing years of the century.

All the novelists discussed in this book were born in the decade 1810–20, except for Disraeli and Surtees who were a few years older and preserved some of the frivolity of an earlier age. The unfrivolous Trollope was the last to die, in 1882. I have concentrated on England—neglecting Trollope's Irish novels—and on writers who are still read, at least in parts, today. Only the more widely-based and 'realistic' novels are relevant: there is not much to be gleaned about Victorian class attitudes from works of fantasy or poetic imagination; from mysteries (like those of Wilkie Collins); from fashionable romances (like Lytton's *Pelham* and

Godolphin); or from stories of well-bred family life (like Charlotte Yonge's *The Heir of Redclyffe*). The same is true of historical novels when (as in *Henry Esmond*) they portray a more or less remote past. But a curiously large number of Victorian novels hark back to the earlier years of the century. Mrs. Gaskell's *Wives and Daughters* recalls the time just before the Reform Bill of 1832; so does George Eliot in *Felix Holt, Middlemarch* and *Mill on the Floss*. These books, though written a generation later, deal with the beginning of my period. Others (*Vanity Fair, Shirley, Sylvia's Lovers, Adam Bede*) go back still further, to the period of the wars with France. Sometimes the mid-Victorians looked back in search of a more colourful and exciting time; sometimes, attracted by the idea of a less complex and industrial society; sometimes because they wanted perspective or (like Thackeray in *Pendennis* and Mrs. Gaskell in *Cranford*) were nostalgic for their youth.[1] Whatever their motives they described a society that observed, basically, the rules of their own day. It was simpler, more predominantly feudal and parochial, less sober and strenuous in tone; but its fabric was the same.

I thought at first that it might be possible to divide Victorian novelists into those who were 'for' and those who were 'against' the system, with others (perhaps chiefly the women novelists) as 'don't knows'. Dickens seemed an obvious opponent and Trollope an obvious champion, with Thackeray both addict and abstainer. But this came to seem too straightforward a distinction. None of the writers accepted the system in its entirety; nor did any of them completely reject it. In the end I thought it better to divide the novelists into:

(i) more or less objective reporters;
(ii) those who dramatized class relations for the sake of reform, revival or comic effect;
(iii) those who, while deliberately and successfully realistic, had an ideal of right conduct which coloured their views on class.

This is, of course, as arbitrary as most divisions. All the novelists treated in this book drew on experience and none of them quite

---

[1] Cf. A. J. P. Taylor, writing of inter-war fiction in his *English History, 1914–1945* (p. 634): 'Most novels are really set twenty or thirty years back, whether avowedly or not.'

lacked objectivity. Most of them had moments of distortion or exaggeration. Some desire to edify was common to all. But the classification is convenient and points to an initial conclusion: that the women novelists are, within the limits of their experience, the most reliable guides to the Victorian social labyrinth. The men know more about the world of action; but their prejudices or ideals distort, or limit, their powers of social observation.

Nobody can read far into Victorian fiction without being struck by the immense importance of being 'gentle'. Most of the novelists had fairly clear ideas of what they meant when they wrote of 'gentlemen' or 'ladies', though they could not define so clearly as they felt. But there was an ambiguity which they never really resolved. Could one be perfectly good without being, in some sense, a 'gentleman'? Could one be a perfect gentleman and yet be bad? Was it social, or moral, vulgarity that really mattered? The novelists' use of the words 'gentleman' and 'lady', whether or not reflecting this central preoccupation, is analysed in a separate chapter.

In a final chapter I touch, briefly, on the way in which the Victorians justified their system. A fuller discussion would open up questions reaching beyond Victorian fiction and too searching for this book.

To set the scene the opening chapter attempts a rapid sketch of Victorian society, as it emerges from the fiction of the time. Here and there the skeleton is filled out with a little non-fictional knowledge. But I have tried to convey the sort of unscientific idea that Victorians formed of their own society (and found reflected in their novels) rather than to complete and analyse it with historical hindsight.

There were of course limits to the novelists' social experience. None of them had an intimate knowledge of the labouring poor, though Mrs. Gaskell had learned a good deal and others—as Disraeli in *Sybil*—could mug up working class conditions when they must. Only Dickens was really at home with the urban lower middle class. Charlotte Brontë was closely limited by her experience as a governess and country parson's daughter. Thackeray knew something of Bohemia and Trollope of Suburbia; but otherwise they seldom strayed very effectively beyond the upper middle class and gentry and those who depended on them. George Eliot spread wider, with a penetrating sympathy and a good knowledge of the rural and provincial middle classes; but there were limits at both ends of her scale. Surtees' range was extensive but shallow: that of an enterprising country gentleman and sporting man who had lived a good deal about town. At the upper end of the scale only Disraeli gives a vivid picture of the fashionable and smart.

Nevertheless, whatever their knowledge of the classes, or their ignorance of the masses, the novelists all knew a good deal about the relations between class and class and class and mass. If they were not always certain exactly how the other half lived and felt, they were at least familiar with the structure that kept them, up or down, in their place. This structure—the ladder rather than the rungs—is the subject of this book.

2. Ordered Estates

Looking back from the middle years of the century novelists could recall a pastoral England, where the country still bulked larger than the towns and where every village was an island. In each distinct community the squire and/or the parson represented the gentry. Below them were the well-to-do farmers and the rural professional men—doctors, lawyers and, more humbly, school-masters. Below them, again, the rural artisans and tradesmen (carpenters, blacksmiths, wheelwrights, saddlers, weavers, shop-keepers) and, finally, the labourers who often lived and ate in the farms where they worked. Where there was a big house the servants would form a community of their own, observing its own hierarchy. The village innkeeper might be (as in *Adam Bede*) a former butler of the squire's. The Parish Clerk helped the Rector to maintain the dignity of the Church, which radiated more or less benevolently, but without excessive heat.

George Eliot brings out most pungently the contrast in village and country town life between the turn of the century and her own time. Her recollections have a gently idyllic glow and convey a touch of nostalgia for patriarchal stability. Perhaps this stability was partly illusory and belonged to a child's world rather than to the actual world of late eighteenth-century England. There was never a time, even in the eighteenth century, when social relations stood still. In so far as they had found a balance it was one that, in the country, lasted substantially until George Eliot's death and even later. She says, writing of 1799 in *Adam Bede*: '. . . in those days the keenest of bucolic minds felt a whispering awe at the sight of the gentry . . .' But this awe was not very much less potent in the middle of the nineteenth century. There were parts of England where it was still to be reckoned with in the twentieth century.

There had certainly been some decline in feudal spirit between the Napoleonic Wars and the mid-Victorian era, but not to a revolutionary extent; the structure of rural society remained basically the same throughout the eighteenth and nineteenth centuries. The real contrast between the countryside of, say 1800 and 1850 lay in material, rather than social, conditions: the greater intensity of cultivation, the greater absorption of the countryside for urban and industrial use, and above all the greater ease of communication. It was the railways, rather than any social revolution, that changed the rural life that George Eliot had glimpsed in her childhood: the theme of the Railway Revolution is a frequent and stirring *leit-motiv* in Victorian fiction. Ease of communication disturbed parochial self-sufficiency and diffused fashions and ideas. Clergymen began to torture themselves and their parishioners with points of doctrine. In refined provincial circles there was a serious striving after culture. Hospitality became more elegant and conversation more virtuous; the well-to-do ate and drank rather less heavily than they had before.

These changes in manners did not affect the social balance of the nation as a whole, so much as did the growth of the towns and of industrial activity. During the period covered in this book England changed from a predominantly rural country to a predominantly urban one. In 1851 the Census showed half the population—which then stood at 18 million—as urban. After this date the population continued to expand rapidly and the large towns became more and more important.

Mrs. Gaskell's *North and South* brings out more sharply than any other novel the contrast between the life of the traditional England and that of the new manufacturing towns. Aristocratic influence was overwhelming in the former, even after the Reform Bill of 1832. In the latter it seldom counted for much, in practical terms, and sometimes for nothing. Wealth and power, rather than gentility, were the standards of the new manufacturing society—as they have been in most parts of the United States and still tend to be in the industrial North today. The working classes may have feared or respected their masters; but they did not owe them a traditional reverence. The masters sometimes treated their men humanely and sometimes not; but their understanding of economic laws (*Hard Times* gives a powerful, if exaggerated, picture of their attitude) tended to put paternalism at a discount.

Disraeli's *Sybil*, published in 1845, set out to startle by announcing the co-existence of two nations in early Victorian England:

'Two nations, between whom there is no intercourse and no sympathy; who are as ignorant of each other's habits, thoughts and feelings, as if they were dwellers in different zones, or inhabitants of different planets; who are formed by a different breeding, are fed by a different food, are ordered by different manners, and are not governed by the same laws.'

Disraeli was referring to the Rich and the Poor—and indeed the difference between an aristocrat and an industrial worker of the time was entirely what he claimed. But there were many sorts of rich and many sorts of poor. Perhaps a truer contrast would have been between the new industrial nation (of all classes) and the older nation which still surrounded it and from which it had sprung.

Much of the wealth and more of the enterprise of the country was concentrated in the industrial towns; but they did not set the social tone. Although the inhabitants of these towns were quick to forget their rural origins, some of the traditional sense of rank was bound to linger. In *Hard Times* Dickens pictures Mrs. Sparsit—a decayed, though majestic, gentlewoman—as malevolently keeping house in an industrial town for the self-made Mr. Bounderby, who deeply appreciates her lady-like qualities. Mr. Gradgrind, the rigid economist, is in league with Mr. Bounderby. We are told that 'the Gradgrind school . . . liked fine gentlemen; they pretended that they did not, but they did. They became exhausted in imitation of them; and they yaw-yawed in their speech like them . . .' Dickens suggests a kind of unholy alliance between manufacturers and aristocrats, in which each tried to make use of the other. The former had wealth and power, in their own sphere, but could not help being impressed by the latter.

Mr. Thornton, the manufacturer in Mrs. Gaskell's *North and South*, has a sturdy independence. He sets little store by the values of 'the South', respects hard work and material success, and boasts that the manufacturing working-man 'may raise himself into the power and position of a master by his own exertions and behaviour'. But he is ready to describe the impoverished Hale family to his mother as 'a gentleman and ladies'. Manufacturers were not necessarily above having their sons educated at aristocratic public schools, even when, like Mr. Millbank in Disraeli's *Coningsby*, they were of a 'democratic bent' and disapproved of them. Their sons or grandsons might use their money, like the returning 'nabobs' of the eighteenth century, to acquire landed property and, with it, social respectability of the older type. Thus Lord Minchampstead, in Kingsley's *Yeast*, was a mill-owner and coal-owner before he became a landed proprietor 'as the summit of his own and his compeers' ambition'; his dissenting, self-made, father had said to him: 'I have made a gentleman of you, you must make a nobleman of yourself.'

If the new manufacturing class was wealthy, the landowners had not yet been hit by the bad harvests and cheap American corn of the seventies and they kept their heads above water in the middle of the nineteenth century. Agriculture was seldom a very paying investment;[1] but owners of non-agricultural land shared in the general prosperity. As to power, the manufacturers certainly enjoyed it in their own towns and businesses, and their needs and attitudes strongly affected national policies. But the government of the countryside, and of the nation as a whole, remained in the hands of the aristocracy and gentry. Rank had perhaps governed society more absolutely in the eighteenth century and had adopted a haughtier style. Thackeray at least was under that impression, when he wrote in *The Virginians* of the middle eighteenth century that 'in those times, when the distinction of ranks yet obtained, to be high and distant with his inferiors, brought no unpopularity to a gentleman'. Lord St. George, in Trollope's *Vicar of Bullhampton*, had moved with the times and would disturb his father by reminding him that 'in these days'—presumably the late sixties—'marquises were not very different from other people, except in this, that they perhaps might have more money.' But, if the manifestations of rank had become more discreet, its superiority was still very widely accepted. Although the intellectual and artistic life of the country was less firmly under aristocratic patronage than it had been in the eighteenth century, landed families still dominated Parliament and London society, as well as their own counties or parishes, and they still set fashions in dress and behaviour. Cobden wrote to a friend in 1858:

'During my experience the higher classes never stood so high in relative social and political rank compared with the other

---

[1] Cf. *English Landed Society in the Nineteenth Century* by F. M. L. Thompson.

classes as at present. The middle classes have been content with the very crumbs from their table . . .'[1]

Thus, in spite of the emergence of new forces and classes, and in spite of the increasing diversity of English life, the old social system continued and flourished. It even reacted to change by developing a greater self-consciousness and rigidity. All readers of mid-Victorian fiction must be impressed by the sense which it conveys of a society both intricate and stable. Even Dickens, who found so much in society to dislike, gives an impression of solidity and permanence in the social order. There was certainly a time, in 'the hungry forties', when novelists became aware of dangerous divisions in society and when the distress, or resentment, of the poor seemed to threaten revolution. This was the time of the 'social protest' novel: Disraeli's *Sybil* (1845), Mrs. Gaskell's *Mary Barton* (1848), Kingsley's *Alton Locke* (1850) and *Yeast* (1851). But the resentment was gradually alleviated by governmental concessions, by the removal of abuses and by greater economic security; Chartism petered out; there was no revolution. By the time of the late fifties and sixties (the period of Trollope's best novels) the essential stability of society seems to be taken for granted in current fiction. There are still abuses to correct; there is still scope for a gradual evolution; but there is no danger of any rapid or drastic overhaul. In *Phineas Redux* Trollope notes that the differences between the two English parliamentary parties are really very small: 'Who desires among us to put down the Queen, or to repudiate the National Debt, or to destroy religious worship, or even to disturb the ranks of society?'

It was in the sixties that Sir Hugo Mallinger, of George Eliot's *Daniel Deronda*, 'carried out his plan of spending part of the autumn at Diplow' and spread

'some cheerfulness in the neighbourhood among all ranks and persons concerned, from the stately homes of Brackenshaw and Quetsham to the respectable shop-parlours in Wancester. For Sir Hugo was a man who liked to show himself and be affable, a

[1] Cf. Robert Blake's *Disraeli* (p. 273): 'As late as 1870 four hundred peers were reckoned to own over one-sixth of the whole surface of the country. It is not surprising that Cabinet and Parliament, lower as well as upper House, were overwhelmingly aristocratic in composition.'

Liberal of good lineage, who confided entirely in Reform as not likely to make any serious difference in English habits of feeling, one of which undoubtedly is the liking to behold society well fenced and adorned with hereditary rank. Hence he made Diplow a most agreeable house, extending his invitations to old Wancester solicitors and young village curates, but also taking some care in the combination of his guests, and not feeding all the common poultry together, so that they should think their meal no particular compliment.'

It is a combination of complexity and stability, of vigour and strict form, that seems to confer on mid-Victorian society its classic quality—the sense that what preceded (however attractive in its simplicity) was a preparation and that what followed (however refreshing in its informality) must be a dissolution.

How much the form was created by the novelists themselves: how much they helped to establish and perpetuate the social distinctions that they portrayed: it is impossible to say. At least the socially conservative Trollope seems likely to have had some influence of this kind. Yet, though his novels may have confirmed his middle-class and upper-class readers in their social attitudes, he was himself obliged to describe a world that was familiar and agreeable to them. In his *Autobiography* he complains about the reception of his novel *Lady Anna*:

'In it a young girl, who is really a lady of high rank and great wealth, though in her youth she enjoyed none of the privileges of wealth or rank, marries a tailor who had been good to her, and whom she had loved when she was poor and neglected. A fine young noble lover is provided for her, and all the charms of sweet living with nice people are thrown in her way, in order that she may be made to give up the tailor. And the charms are very powerful with her. But the feeling that she is bound by her troth to the man who had always been true to her overcomes everything —and she marries the tailor. It was my wish of course to justify her in doing so, and to carry my readers along with me in my sympathy with her. But everybody found fault with me for marrying her to the tailor.'

It would be unfair not to continue the quotation. Trollope goes on to say: 'What would they have said if I had allowed her to jilt the tailor and marry the good-looking young lord?' The most satisfactory solution would presumably have been for the tailor to die, or to perform a heroic act of self-renunciation, leaving the girl free to marry her noble lover with a clear conscience. But, in *Lady Anna*, Trollope was too much of a realist for that. As it was, he recognized, with truth, that Victorian sentiment called for as much nourishment as Victorian snobbery. Coronets were important; but so, in a different, and no doubt more basic, way were kind hearts. So much was this so, that the Victorian might even need to be reassured that, *pace* Dickens, 'Hearts just as brave and fair may beat in Belgrave Square as in the lowly air of Seven Dials'[1] or, as Thackeray puts it in *Philip*: 'Because people are rich, they are not of necessity ogres. Because they are gentlemen and ladies of good degree, are in easy circumstances, and have a generous education, it does not follow that they are heartless and will turn their back on a friend.'

In all that follows it has to be remembered that, for most Victorians, inequality on earth was to be completed or compensated by a different kind of inequality after death. Rank conferred its temporary distinction; but equality in the sight of God would ensure that, in the long run, virtue met with its reward. The intelligent Lady Harriet, in Mrs. Gaskell's *Wives and Daughters*, is very conscious of her position and apt to be a bit disdainful of some of her inferiors. But she tells Molly Gibson: 'I don't set myself up in solid things as any better than my neighbours.'

*   *   *

At the top of the social structure there was, of course, the Royal Family. There are some rather unkind references, particularly in Thackeray, to the inglorious figure cut, and the poor moral example set, by George IV. There is a dazzling picture in *Sybil* of Queen Victoria's accession to the throne. But both respect and ignorance prevented the Victorian novelists from attempting intimate revelations of Court life. For practical purposes their

[1] W. S. Gilbert: *Iolanthe* (1882).

social world is dominated by the titled aristocracy, culminating in Dukes.

'Dukes? What does Ben know about Dukes?' This question of Disraeli *père* could have been asked about most Victorian writers, when there were so few real Dukes available for study. It does not prevent the appearance of quite a sprinkling of Dukes and Duchesses in their novels, whether close-up (like Trollope's two Dukes of Omnium) or in crowd scenes, like the Duchess of Menteith in *Wives and Daughters*, whose toilette *a l'enfant* at the Hollingford charity ball created so much disappointment. There is no dearth, either, of Marquesses, Earls, Viscounts and Barons. The Marquess of Monmouth in *Coningsby* (perhaps Disraeli's most life-like creature and, like Lord Steyne in *Vanity Fair*, based on the real character of Lord Hertford) epitomizes class arrogance when he meets his grandson's political scruples with the words: 'You go with your family, sir, like a gentleman; you are not to consider your opinions, like a philosopher or a political adventurer' and 'I tell you what it is, Harry, members of this family may think as they like, but they must act as I please'. The older Duke of Omnium has something of this self-sufficiency, in a muted form; but most of the fictional aristocrats later in the century are less splendidly immune from altruism and self-doubt. Indeed another of Disraeli's peers, Lord Montfort in *Endymion*, who has all Lord Monmouth's grand selfishness though his tastes are quieter, appears as a survival from another age: he was 'the only living Englishman who gave one an idea of the nobleman of the 18th Century.'

Towards the lower end of the aristocracy the Baronetcy appears in an unusual light in *Sybil*, where Sir Vavasour Firebrace describes his order to the politely incredulous Egremont as '. . . a military order, sir, if properly understood . . . Evidently the body destined to save this country. Blending all sympathies: the crown of which they are the peculiar champions; the nobles of whom they are the popular branch; the people who recognize in them their natural leaders.' Sir Vavasour has no luck with Lady Joan Fitz-Warene. 'A baronetcy has become the distinction of the middle class', she tells him, 'a physician, our physician for example, is a baronet; and I dare say some of our tradesmen; brewers, or people of that class. An attempt to elevate them into an order of nobility, however inferior, would partake, in some degree, of the ridiculous.' Nevertheless Miss Aylmer, daughter of a north country baronet in Trollope's *The Belton Estate*, is firmly aristocratic and sustains herself in a dreary life with the consciousness of being so. She prayed God to 'make her humble in the high position to which it had pleased Him to call her . . . She taught the little children in the parish, being specially urgent to them always to courtesy when they saw any of the family . . .'

The uncertainties with which foreign aristocracies have had to contend did not distract the English nobility, firmly ranked in an established order of precedence. But, while recognizing this precedence, the novelists tended to draw a general distinction between Whig magnates on the one hand, wealthy and grand, with cultivated and cosmopolitan tastes and of relatively recent lineage; and, on the other, Tory peers of ancient family, usually less grand and articulate, but in some rather obscure way incarnating national and traditional virtues. This bias would be at its most blatant in Disraeli, if it were not that few of his titled families can claim ancient lineage at all. It is noticeable in Trollope, for all his liberalism in politics, and reflects the instinctive admiration felt by most of the novelists, and their readers, for old family. The Dowager Lady Chettam says of her baronet son in *Middlemarch*: 'James' title is worth far more than any new earldom. I never wished his father to be anything else than Sir James.' Thackeray betrays a touch of genealogical romanticism in *Vanity Fair* when he describes Lady Steyne's family, the Caerlyons, 'whose pedigree goes far beyond the date of the arrival of King Brute in these islands', still attached to the old faith and suffering from a 'mysterious taint of the blood'. Usually, however, a good Saxon or Norman pedigree will do. In *Wives and Daughters* Lady Harriet rather shocks her mother, Lady Cumnor, by recalling that the untitled Hamleys 'have been on their land since before the Conquest; while we only came into the country a century ago; and there is a tale that the first Cumnor began his fortune through selling tobacco in King James' reign.' But Mrs. Gibson is not impressed when her stepdaughter makes the same point to her: 'Now, Molly, I can't have you democratic. Rank is a great distinction. It is quite enough to have dear papa with democratic tendencies.'

Ranking next to the nobility, the landed gentry—without the

distinction of title, though frequently (like the Hamleys) of older blood—might dispute with the commercial middle class and the yeoman farmers of Old England the claim to be the backbone of the country. The 1848 Introduction to Burke's *Genealogical and Heraldic Dictionary of the Landed Gentry* described the gentry as

'that class in Society which holds the next place to the privileged Order—the untitled Country Gentlemen—a class, though, be it remembered, not one degree below the other, in antiquity of descent, personal accomplishment, and national usefulness; nay, the Chiefs of the Houses from which the Nobility spring, are generally to be found in this division of the Aristocracy, and for the simple reason, that the eldest son and heir being already provided for, the field of adventure belongs, almost exclusively, to the junior members of the family, who, thus forced upon the arena, achieve, by their prowess or their talents—the sword or the pen—fame, wealth, and eminence.'

There are of course numerous country gentlemen in Victorian fiction and, as a class, they are sympathetically treated. Sometimes their sons do achieve eminence, like the scientific Roger Hamley. For themselves, they live on their estates, shoot and hunt, take an interest in farming and their tenantry, occasionally visit London, engage in politics, study law, dabble in letters. Surtees, observing in *Ask Mamma* that '. . . the world proceeds on the aspiring scale, each man looking to the class a little in advance of his own', claims that the happiest are 'the sporting country gentlemen who live at home at ease', free from the anxieties of the great and money-making yet 'sufficiently informed and refined to be the companions of either', living with nature, envying nobody and comfortably exempt from the need to keep up appearances. In his *Book of Snobs* Thackeray admits that snobbishness is not to be found in genuine, stupid and honourable county families. 'Perhaps we do not respect an ox. We rather acquiesce in him.'

The upper clergy, particularly in the earlier part of the century, were often sprung from the nobility and gentry. Disraeli notes in *Tancred* that it was only after the Napoleonic wars that 'it began to be discerned that the time had gone by, at least in England, for bishoprics to serve as appanages for the younger sons of great

families.' Bishops and Deans took a distinguished place in
Society; Canons and Rectors of good livings were eminently
respectable;[1] curates—and of course dissenting clergymen—were
distinctly less grand. However, clergymen of the established
church, whether or not marked out for preferment, were normally
expected to be 'gentlemen', at least by education. Alton Locke's
cousin thought there were only two ways for a young plebeian to
become a gentleman—one was to join a heavy cavalry regiment and
the other was to go to a university and take orders. 'If you are once
a parson, all is safe. Be you who you may before, from that moment
you are a gentleman . . . good enough for any man's society.' The
Rev. Amos Barton in George Eliot's *Scenes of Clerical Life* was a
rather sad case of a decent man with whom the formula had not
quite worked; but then he was an ill-paid curate, without either
the breeding or the scholarship of that other ill-paid curate, Mr.
Crawley in *The Last Chronicle of Barset*.

Kingsley was himself a clergyman. Charlotte Brontë's father
was a country parson who, though born into a peasant (Irish)
family, had been educated at Cambridge and had acquired a certain grandeur of manner. She is merciless in her treatment of
curates, but quite kind to their seniors, in *Shirley*. Clerics, both
eminent and obscure, abound in Trollope's Barchester novels and
in his *Vicar of Bullhampton*, strikingly depicted in their secular
moods, though he disclaimed any personal experience of life in a
Cathedral Close.

In the religious agitations of the early Victorian period clergymen of all types found themselves in the front line and tended to

---

[1] 'There is a class of country clergymen in England, of whom Mr. Clavering was one, and his son-in-law, Mr. Fielding, another, which is so closely
allied to the squirearchy as to possess a double identity. Such clergymen are
not only clergymen, but they are country gentlemen also. Mr. Clavering
regarded clergymen of his class—of the country-gentlemen class, as being
quite distinct from all others—and as being, I may say, very much higher than
all others, without reference to any money question. When meeting his
brother rectors and vicars, he had quite a different tone in addressing them—
as they might belong to his class, or to another. There was no offence in this.
The clerical country-gentlemen understood it all as though there were some
secret sign or shibboleth between them; but the outsiders had no complaint
to make of arrogance, and did not feel themselves aggrieved.' (Trollope:
The Claverings)

26

benefit from a 'black-coat fever' which had replaced the 'red-coat fever' of the Napoleonic Wars. But their social prestige was rooted in earlier centuries. Lady Amelia de Courcy in Trollope's *Doctor Thorne* observed that 'Clergymen—particularly the rectors and vicars of country parishes—do become privileged above other professional men.' They trailed clouds, if not of mediaeval glory, at least of eighteenth-century patronage and prosperity.

The Church was still prominent in scholarship and education. As the tailor Crossthwaite says in *Alton Locke*, the parsons had 'the monopoly of education in England and they get their bread by it at their public schools and universities.' Clergymen were appointed to the headmasterships of public schools and, before the late fifties, all Oxford and Cambridge dons were obliged to take orders. Mr. Bell of Oxford, in Mrs. Gaskell's *North and South*, is a good-natured example. Thus the clerical class was very much at the centre of the 'established' intellectual life of the nation and contributed largely to the growth of the 'intellectual aristocracy' which became increasingly influential as the century wore on. Clerical families of this type provided a main source of recruits for the professions and services, though these were also manned by the minor gentry and by some aspirants from below.

Civil service appointments were based entirely on patronage in the earlier part of the period: it was because of his mother's friendship with the daughter-in-law of the head of the Post Office that Trollope himself was given a job in the Secretary's office of the G.P.O. in 1834. A rather jaundiced caricature of the results of this system appears in Dickens's picture of the Circumlocution Office in *Little Dorrit*: the Department exists for the benefit of the Barnacle family, not of the nation—its energies (such as they are) are devoted to keeping the public at bay. In Thackeray's *Philip* neither Mr. Twysden, of the Powder and Pomatum Office, nor Mr. Ringwood, who is very exclusive socially and patronizes his chief, seem greatly oppressed by their official duties, while there is a delightful air of leisure in the Chancery of the Paris Embassy. Trollope's *Three Clerks* contrasts the new-style, hard-working, 'Weights and Measures Office' ('exactly antipodistic of the Circumlocution Office') with more slovenly and traditional Government departments. By no means all clerks in Government Departments, whether new-style or old-style, were as gilded as Mr.

Ringwood. Mr. Dosett, the Admiralty clerk in Trollope's *Ayala's Angel*, lives in genteel poverty at Notting Hill Gate on his £900 a year and he and his wife have no social life at all. This was in the seventies; but, even when patronage flourished, it did not necessarily confer social distinction. Senior officials might enjoy some prestige; Private Secretaries and diplomatists were often smart; but the more obscure members of the bureaucracy, though respectable, were dim. However, at a less educated level, there was still some scope for insolence of office: Mr. Lillyrick, the collector of water rates in *Nicholas Nickleby*, had a tremendous position in his own circle as 'a public man'.

The Army—and to a lesser extent the Navy—remained something of an aristocratic preserve, but less so in the less 'dandy' regiments. As Thackeray's novels show, the purchase of commissions did not prevent the growth of a professional officer class, drawn from the lesser gentry and middle class, who found opportunities for promotion in India. Thus Mrs. Baynes in *Philip* could be a 'general officer's lady' and yet be vulgarity itself. The merchant navy was of course socially inferior to the Royal Navy. Mr. Fountain in Charles Reade's *Love me Little, Love me Long* describes young Mr. Dodd as 'what I call a nondescript—like an attorney, or a surgeon, or a civil engineer, or a banker, or a stockbroker, and all that sort of people . . . Old families don't go into the merchant-service. Indeed it would not answer. There they rise by—by—mere maritime considerations.'

Medicine had its prizes, though it was better to be a rich doctor's son, like Prime Minister Addington, than to be a practising doctor, and even then the aura of the consulting room took a good deal of living down. 'As to *mesalliance*, there's no blood on any side' says Lady Pentreath in *Daniel Deronda*: 'Old Admiral Arrowpoint was one of Nelson's men, you know—a doctor's son. And we all know how the mother's money came.' (It came through trade.) Sir Vavasour Firebrace in *Sybil* complains of a fellow baronet: '. . . he was for compromise, but d—— him, his father was only an accoucheur.'

The Bar had yet more glittering prizes and was as a rule more gentlemanly. Sprigs of the country gentry, like Warrington in *Pendennis* or Surtees himself, could read law, live in chambers and do some scribbling without aiming at the heights of their profession. Those who did aim at its heights had to be able and hard-working, since the competition was fierce. According to Trollope (in *The Bertrams*): 'Senior wranglers and double-firsts, when not possessed of means for political life, usually find their way to the bar.' By contrast engineering, a more recent career, was more exclusively for the self-made; the narrator's father in Mrs. Gaskell's *Cousin Phyllis* is a good example.[1] Journalism, too, was quite compatible with dropped aitches (Mr. Mugford in *Philip* drops them liberally), though Trollope's Tom Towers maintained the dignity of *The Times*. In *He knew he was right*, the Bohemian Hugh Stanbury is disapproved of by his aunt and by his prospective in-laws because he writes for a penny newspaper. According to his friend Trevelyan, in leaving the bar for journalism, 'he was sinking from the highest to almost the lowest business by which an educated man and a gentleman could earn his bread.'

Successful professional and official men could, without pene-trating the nobility, improve their social position and their place at table by becoming knighted. In *Ask Mamma* the belief that Crickleton's father, an eminent chiropodist, *might* have been knigh-ted confers prestige on him in the drab society of his country neighbourhood: 'Though the Major used, when in the running-down tack, to laugh at the idea of a knight's son claiming pre-cedence, yet, when on the running-up one, he used to intimate that his friend's father might have been knighted, and even sometimes assigned the honour to his friend himself.'

Although the gulf was wide between the professional class and the nobility or upper gentry, their children could be educated at the same schools or universities and the way to social and political advancement was open to the successful lawyer or doctor who had made money. Even the poor and unsuccessful among them could regard themselves as gentlemen and, when they had been educated as such, others would normally do so too. The use of this vital, but disputed, title was a good deal more doubtful in the moneyed strata of the middle class.

Whatever merchants might feel, 'trade' was incompatible with

[1] Cf. Chapter LII of *Endymion*: 'Civil engineering was then (*c*. 1840) beginning to attract general attention and Lord Montfort liked the society of civil engineers; but what he liked most were self-formed men, and to learn the secret of their success and how they made their fortune.'

29

gentility. In spite of the value which all classes placed on wealth, this Platonic maxim was applied with surprising firmness. Very rich men, like Mr. Melmotte in Trollope's *The Way We Live Now*, or Mr. Merdle in Dickens's *Little Dorrit*, could flourish their real or reputed wealth as if they were aristocrats, but they could not buy blood. Until later in the century it was hard enough for them to buy social success. Surtees exclaims: 'Mr. Prospero Plutus may gild his coach and his harness, and his horses too, if he likes, but all the lacquer in the world will not advance him a step in society.' Later in the century this was less true. The elderly Disraeli, in *Endymion*, noticed 'the successful invasions of society by new classes' and recalled that: 'Forty years ago the great financiers had not that commanding, not to say predominant position in society which they possess at present.'

Vanity Fair deals with the beginning of the century. Mr. Osborne, the well-to-do City merchant, calls himself a gentleman but seems to know that he is not; he invites professional people to his dinners and is determined that his son should be brought up as the real thing. That was one resource for the social climber. Another was to contrive an aristocratic marriage. 'I am of a savage and envious nature', says Thackeray in *The Book of Snobs*, 'I like to see these two humbugs (race and wealth) which, dividing as they do, the social empire of this kingdom between them, hate each other naturally—making truce and uniting—for the sordid interests of either.' In the same vein he notes that the City Snob's money gets washed after an aristocratic marriage and becomes 'real aristocratic coin.'

Marriages between the Court and the City were of course no new thing (Mrs. Gaskell's Lady Ludlow thought they had weakened the aristocracy's sense of smell) and it was a far cry from the Toryism of the older type of City merchant to the sturdy provincialism of the new manufacturing class. Businessmen of this new type were much more apt to scorn genteel values. In return their vulgarity and brutal insistence on wealth invited the disdain not only of the gentry but of the professional class. Provincial industrialists were hardly regarded as gentlemen—unless, which was unusual, they happened to be gentlemanly by birth or education—but they did not necessarily care. They lived in their own world, were proud of their own achievements and tended to look down

on more effete classes and districts—at least until they had made
enough money to think of entering Parliament or sending their
sons to Eton.

In the countryside the ambitions of prosperous farmers were
inevitably cast in a traditional mould. During the Napoleonic
Wars many members of the old yeoman class, who owned their
own farms and gloried in not paying rent, had worked their way
up into the minor gentry. Although yeomen were increasingly
regarded as an extinct species,[1] the process to some extent continued. John Hybrid illustrates it in *Ask Mamma*. He builds a
lodge and adds a portico to his farm, puts on a blue roof, advertises
in the local Gazette that he is to be addressed as 'Esquire' and his
house known as 'Hall', grows an imperial and when hunting
'mounts the pink'. (When Miss de Glancey marries him she
removes his plate from the drawing-room, where it had been
proudly displayed, and gets him into Burke's *Landed Gentry*.)
Similarly in *Pendennis* 'Mr. Hobnell's father pulled down the old
farmhouse; built a flaring new whitewashed mansion, with
capacious stables; and a piano in the drawing-room; kept a pack
of harriers; and assumed the title of Squire Hobnell. When he died
and his son reigned in his stead, the family might be fairly considered to be established as country gentry.' On the other hand
Mr. Cheesacre in Trollope's *Can You Forgive Her?*, although he
owns his own land and is comfortably off, describes himself as 'a
poor Norfolk farmer. I never want to put myself beyond my own
place. There has been some talk about the Commission of the
Peace, but I don't think anything of it.' Similar, though more
firm-minded, self-denial had been shown much earlier in the century by Miss Pole's cousin, in *Cranford*, who lived on his own estate
'but his property was not large enough to entitle him to rank
higher than a yeoman; or rather, with something of the "pride
which apes humility", he had refused to push himself on, as so
many of his class had done, into the ranks of the squires. He would
not allow himself to be called Thomas Holbrook Esq.; he
even sent back letters with this address, telling the post-mistress

[1] Cf. Trollope's *The American Senator*: '. . . there were in the country
round sundry yeomen, as they ought to be called,—gentlemen-farmers as
they now like to style themselves,—men who owned some acres of land, and
farmed these acres themselves.'

at Cranford that his name was Mr. Thomas Holbrook, yeoman.'

The yeomen Dodsons, in *Mill on the Floss*, though virtually uneducated, have as rigid a sense of family as any aristocratic clan. Tenant farmers, like Mr. Poyser in *Adam Bede*, were in a different category; but they too might be comfortably off and hold their heads high. George Eliot is the novelist most at home in this world, though her descriptions are of a generation or more ago. She also has a sure touch with her provincial professional men. They are usually a cut below their metropolitan colleagues; it was perhaps particularly of country solicitors that Mrs. Gaskell's Lady Cumnor was thinking when, disdaining the vital difference between a barrister and an 'attorney',[1] she said: 'although there is a general prejudice against attorneys, I have known two or three who are very respectable men . . .' The Rev. John Lingon regards the provincial lawyer Jermyn, in *Felix Holt*, as 'one of your middle-class upstarts who want to rank with gentlemen, and think they'll do it with kid gloves and new furniture.' Lady Cumnor is even more damning about land agents (like George Eliot's father): 'I never think whether a land-agent is handsome or not. They don't belong to the class of people whose appearance I notice.' In *Ask Mamma* the land and mining agents, together with the auditor, the architect, the builder and the doctor, make up the satellites 'of the second class' who are the first guests to arrive for the big Hunt breakfast at Tantivy Hall.

From this point downwards there is no pretence at gentility, though there are still important social gradations. In the country-side, the tradespeople and skilled artisans (like—or unlike—Adam Bede and Felix Holt) are naturally distinct from the mass of ordinary farm labourers. The novelists discussed in this book tell us little about the thoughts and feelings of the lowest class of agricultural workers, though they use them to supply touches of bucolic colour in the background. Kingsley was much concerned with the living conditions of the peasants, but never really succeeds in introducing them as individuals. He has more affection for the independent Cornish fishermen of Aberalva, who 'are on their own ground, and know it; who will not touch their caps to

---

[1] Cf. Trollope in *The Last Chronicle of Barset*: 'It may be observed that ladies belonging to the families of solicitors always talk about lawyers and never about attorneys or barristers.'

you, or pull the short black pipe from between their lips as you pass, but expect you to prove yourself a gentleman by speaking respectfully to them.'

The lower urban scene is richer. For the lower middle class there is Dickens's marvellous and extensive gallery of clerks, shop-keepers, undertakers, nurses and minor functionaries. Lower middle-class characters, such as commercial travellers, bailiffs and detectives (very far removed cousins of the Wimseys and Alleyns of this century!), also appear in Trollope, though usually in brief and rather class-conscious glimpses. There is, for instance, Mr. Clarkson, the dunn in *Phineas Finn*: 'The old man in the white cravat was very neatly dressed, and carried himself without any of that humility which betrays one class of uncertified aspirants to gentility, or of that assumed arrogance which is at once fatal to another class. But, nevertheless, Mrs. Bunce had seen at a glance that he was not a gentleman . . .'

Detailed accounts of industrial working-class life are largely confined to the novels of social protest (*Mary Barton, Sybil, Hard Times*). Hence working-class characters tend to be idealized either into the honest and right-feeling, or into the bitter and opiniona-ted, or into the drunken and useless. In any case most of their talk is oppressively artificial because delicacy is always paramount. (For the same reason, of course, Thackeray and Trollope, though very much men of the world, were obliged to skirt extremely carefully round the subject of physical sex.) Nevertheless Mrs. Gaskell shows real sympathy and some real insight in her pictures of factory hands and their families. Job Legh in *Mary Barton* is a fine example of a recognizable Victorian type: the intelligent, serious-minded, working man, with scientific interests. In *Shirley* Joe Scott claims intelligence of this kind as a Northern characteristic: 'I reckon 'at us manufacturing lads i' the north is a good deal more intelligent, and knows a deal more nor th' farming folk i' th' south.'

The lower class, both urban and rural, supplied the vast corps of servants required by the upper and middle classes, though upper servants (butlers, housekeepers and ladies' maids) enjoyed lower middle-class status and might become impressively genteel. Aylmer Park, in Trollope's *The Belton Estate*, belongs to a baronet with a dominating wife, determined to maintain the family's position in the county: 'It required a great many servants to keep it in order, and the numerous servants required an experienced duenna, almost as grand in appearance as Lady Aylmer herself, to keep them in order. There was an open carriage and a close carriage, and a butler, and two footmen, and three gamekeepers, and four gardeners, and there was a coachman, and there were grooms, and sundry inferior men and boys about the place to do the work which the gardeners and gamekeepers and grooms did not choose to do themselves. And they all became fat, and lazy, and stupid, and respectable together; so that, as the reader will at once perceive, Aylmer Park was kept up in the proper British style.' There are good pictures of 'gentlemen's gentlemen' and also of less distinguished servants, in Thackeray, Dickens and Surtees. Governesses were of course better born and educated; Charlotte Brontë had herself smarted under the humiliations that they were expected to endure. Mrs. Pryor in *Shirley* recalls being told by the aristocratic Miss Hardman that 'Governesses . . . must ever be kept in a sort of isolation.' In Miss Hardman's view providence had arranged for a number of imprudent fathers to supply the aristocracy with lady-like governesses, since the 'daughters of tradespeople, however well-educated, must necessarily be under-bred, and as such unfit to be inmates of OUR dwellings or guardians of OUR children's minds and persons.'

Private soldiers and able seamen were also recruited from the lower class; their uniforms conferred some glamour, but little social prestige. Sailors always enjoyed a kind of popularity in the days when Britannia ruled the waves; but the army was less favoured and, later in the century, Kipling had to work quite hard to establish the private soldier in his countrymen's esteem. Another type of glamour without prestige—always attended, in Victorian fiction, with eventual ruin—was to be found in the underworld of thieves and prostitutes which figures in *Oliver Twist*.

One social class was difficult to place. Literature was an occupation for a gentleman; but there were naturally writers who were not gentlemen. An occasional portrait painter might pass; but, as a general rule, an artistic, musical or dramatic career was as difficult to combine with gentility as trade. Herr Klessmer, in *Daniel Deronda*, whose great musical genius we have to take on trust, is regarded by the conventional Mr. Bult as a 'mere musician' and the Arrowpoints are horrified at the prospect of his marrying their daughter. Mr. Sympson in *Shirley* dreads his niece's love falling on 'a low clerk, a play-actor, a playwriter' or indeed on 'any literary scrub, or shabby, whining artist'. In commercial circles artistic stock was particularly low. Old Mr. Osborne in *Vanity Fair* was surprised at one of his married daughter's soirees to see a Lord 'speak to a dam fiddler—a fellar I despise'. He was still more savage, because less certain, about 'parsons, scholars, and the like,—declaring that they were a pack of humbugs, and quacks, that weren't fit to get their living but by grinding Latin and Greek, and a set of supercilious dogs, that pretended to look down upon British merchants and gentlemen, who could buy up half a hundred of 'em.' However, some artists and fiddlers might have the entree to circles where no Osbornes, and for that matter few parsons, would have been admitted. The more cultivated members of the aristocracy took pleasure in patronizing artists, though they would no more than the Arrowpoints have wished their daughters to marry them. Lady Cumnor held that '. . . high rank should always be the first to honour those who have distinguished themselves by art or science.' Lord Eskdale, in *Coningsby*, 'patronised and appreciated the fine arts, though a jockey; respected literary men, though he only read French novels; and without any affectation of tastes which he did not possess, was looked upon by every singer and dancer in Europe as their natural champion'.

Wealth had to admit the claims of Birth, if only because so much power, and often fortune, was still attached to it. Birth, though in principle grandly self-sufficient, had to recognize the utility of wealth. Education and Culture could be valued by Wealth as a means of power and position and by Birth as a part of its way of life. But, when not specifically aimed at power or comfort, the serious pursuit of literature, scholarship, science and the fine arts was difficult to reconcile with some prevailing social values. Even more than Religion, which could always be referred to another world, if it conflicted with this one, it seemed to raise doubts about the proper ordering of society. Hence the difficulty of placing artists and the like—including novelists, until they had made money. Hence the touch of the 'outsider' which appears from time to time in Dickens and Thackeray.

3. Experience

George Eliot and Charlotte Brontë were such unusual women that it may seem crude to classify them as 'women novelists'. But they both display, with Mrs. Gaskell, a realism and a delicacy in their treatment of personal relations, that the men novelists, with their stronger and rougher effects, only occasionally achieve. Their realism was of course limited by their experience. Charlotte Brontë's experience was exceptionally limited—and concentrated; Mrs. Gaskell's was wider, but still that of a Victorian wife and mother; George Eliot had lived more freely, but not so freely as a man. Their movements being more restricted, their observation of what was close to them was sharper, while their interest in people tended to be less coloured by general preconceptions about life.

In Victorian novels women are at once more snobbish, and less snobbish, than men. On the one hand their gentleness and sympathy soften class barriers; on the other hand, when they have class prejudices, these tend to be very exacting. Here again, the comparatively narrow sphere in which Victorian women lived explains a good deal. It fell to them to dress the altar and sweep the hearth; to form social circles and cherish family feeling. Their menfolk, engaged in business and mixing in the world, were harder put to preserve intact the rigidity of their prejudices. Women were the priestesses of the social system; by and large, they had more leisure for it and the men found this convenient. As soon as their sympathies were engaged, however, they were quicker than men to regard people as individuals rather than social types.

There is thus a blend of expertise and neutrality in the approach of the women novelists towards class differences. They seldom distort or exaggerate these differences and are usually content to allow their readers to experience, without too much editorial management, what they have experienced themselves.

*   *   *

The Rev. Patrick Brontë, the father of CHARLOTTE BRONTË, was the son of a peasant-farmer in County Down.

Under the encouragement of the local Rector he was educated at St. John's College, Cambridge and—taking the classic way of advancement open to a poor, clever, boy—entered the Church. He married into a family of rather higher social status: Mrs. Brontë (*née* Branwell) came from respectable Methodist stock in Penzance and had a small annuity.

Mr. Brontë's views, in common with those of most Church of England clergymen of the time, were staunchly Tory. He seems to have done his best to improve his own antecedents. In her *Life of Charlotte Brontë* Mrs. Gaskell refers to a family tradition that they were in fact descended from 'an ancient family'. Mr. Brontë invented the spelling of his name (which had previously been Brunty); he was proud of an acquaintance with Lord Palmerston at Cambridge and he apparently boasted to Mary Burder, an early flame, of his 'great and affluent friends', while concealing his own birth from her.[1]

Charlotte inherited from her father an intense admiration for the Duke of Wellington. When she was 15 she fought a radical school-fellow on behalf of the Duke and against Reform; all her life she remained his devoted partisan. Against this background it is not surprising that there should be an undercurrent of Toryism in Charlotte Brontë's novels. Her heroine Shirley (supposed to be partly based on her sister Emily) feels for the poor in their sufferings, but exclaims:

'If once the poor gather and rise in the form of a mob, I shall turn against them as an aristocrat . . . I shall quite forget pity for their wretchedness and respect for their poverty, in scorn of their ignorance and wrath at their insolence.'

This is not of course the author speaking herself, any more than when, with pronounced irony, she makes the timid Mrs. Pryor say: '. . . the aristocracy are decidedly a very superior class, you know—both physically, and morally, and mentally—as a high Tory I acknowledge that. . . .' But, if she does not quite share Shirley's sentiments, she does not wholly reject them.

The Tory bias appears more directly in a disposition to value old family and in a preoccupation with gentility in physical type.

[1] *The Brontës* by I. Cooper Willis: p. 30

Thus the Rivers family in *Jane Eyre*, who are lovingly portrayed, 'wor gentry i' thi' owd days o' th 'Henrys.' Mr. Rochester, for all his unlikely passion for Jane, is irreproachably county. Mr. Yorke in *Shirley* and Mr. Yorke Hunsden in *The Professor* (two aspects of the same person) both take pride in their rough speech and in their radical views; but they are both, in fact, highly educated Northern gentlemen of old family. Scornful as the latter 'professed to be of the advantages of birth, in his secret heart he well knew and fully appreciated the distinction his ancient, if not high lineage conferred on him in a mushroom-place like X (a manufacturing town) concerning whose inhabitants it was proverbially said that not one in a thousand knew his own grandfather'. The former tacitly confesses his family pride to Shirley, when he tells her: 'Moore is a gentleman. His blood is pure and ancient as mine or thine.'

Mrs. Pryor, in *Shirley*, recalls the portrait of her child, Caroline, at the age of 8: 'there, under the silver paper, I saw blooming the delicacy of an aristocratic flower—"little lady" was written on every trait.' Sir Philip Nunneley has 'the English gentleman in all his deportment'; Dr. John in *Villette* is 'a true young English gentleman'. This is the sort of language in which, in a letter of 1839 quoted in Mrs. Gaskell's *Life*, Charlotte Brontë described one of her employers: 'As he strolled on through his fields, with his magnificent Newfoundland dog at his side, he looked very like what a frank, wealthy Conservative gentleman ought to be.'

The hero of *The Professor*, William Crimsworth, rebels against the aristocratic relatives of his dead mother, who propose to arrange a respectable marriage and a Church living for him, and decides to follow his father into trade. But his plebeian elder brother, who gives him employment, resents his Southern accent and Etonian education and treats him like an insignificant clerk. William, who takes after his mother's family in appearance, eventually decides that trade is not for him (though he has a very bourgeois sense of the virtues of self-help)—and in the end sends his own son to Eton. The radical Yorke Hunsden tells him:

'What a nobleman you would have made, William Crimsworth! You are cut out for one; pity Fortune has baulked Nature! Look at the features, figure, even to the hands—distinction all over—ugly distinction! Now, if you'd only an estate and a mansion, and a park, and a title, how you could play the exclusive, maintain the rights of your class, train your tenantry in habits of respect to the peerage, oppose at every step the advancing power of the people, support your rotten order and be ready for its sake to wade knee-deep in churls' blood. . . .'

When Crimsworth and Hunsden first meet they have a conversation which, besides bringing out the breeding of the one and the inverted snobbery of the other, indicates their creator's rather complex interest in aristocratic type. Hunsden admires the appearance of thought in the portrait of Crimsworth's mother, but goes on to criticize:

'. . . it wants character and force; there's too much of the sen-si-tive . . . in that mouth; besides there is Aristocrat written on the brow and defined in the figure; I hate your aristocrats.'

'You think, then, Mr. Hunsden, that patrician descent may be read in a distinctive cast of form and features?'

'Patrician descent be hanged. Who doubts that your lordlings may have their distinctive "cast of form and features" as much as we ———shire tradesmen have ours? But which is best? Not theirs assuredly. As to their women, it is a little different; they cultivate beauty from childhood upwards, and may by care and training attain to a certain degree of excellence in that point, just like the Oriental odalisques. Yet even this superiority is doubtful.'

(Hunsden's views bring to mind that the other Yorke, in *Shirley*, in spite of his old family, did not have 'a Norman line anywhere; it was an inelegant, unclassic, unaristocratic, mould of visage . . .')

We are meant to sympathize with William Crimsworth, who has some of the characteristics of a masculine Charlotte Brontë. In spite of Hunsden's strictures his aristocratic figure gives him prestige and makes him more interesting to the reader. But his grand connections, the Seacombes, are coldly repellent. For all her instinctive Toryism Charlotte Brontë seems to have felt a kind of resentment against the great and smart, which must partly have been due to her own experiences as a governess and perhaps partly to the understandable failure of aristocrats (other than the Iron

Duke) to realize her ideal. She cannot indeed have had much experience of 'good' society. The conversation between the two Ingrams in *Jane Eyre*, which so much shocked Mrs. Humphrey Ward[1] by its solecisms, is painfully, or ludicrously, artificial. But Miss Brontë knew the girls whom she had to teach at Madame Heger's school in Brussels and there is some middle-class tartness in the judgement in *Villette*:

'Equality is much practised in Labassecour; though not republican in form, it is nearly so in substance, and at the desks of Madame Beck's establishment the young countess and the young bourgeoise sat side by side. Nor could you always by outward indications decide which was noble and which plebeian; except that, indeed, the latter had often franker and more courteous manners . . .'

Perhaps at bottom, Charlotte Brontë's social bias was neither peasant nor aristocratic—neither inherited from her father's ancestors, nor shaped by his or her pretensions or romantic leanings. When she looks at the ranks above her it is with the clear, hard, slightly jealous, gaze of a *bourgeoise*, determined to maintain independence of judgement and to assess glitter at its real worth. In this mood she seems to use the eyes of Methodism and Penzance—perhaps the eyes of her mother's sister who for nearly twenty years made Haworth Parsonage her home. There was certainly a Puritanism in her make-up which inclined her to take a severe view of society. She admired Thackeray's satire and compared him, most inappropriately, to a denunciatory figure from the Old Testament in her dedication of *Jane Eyre*:

'I have alluded to him, Reader, because I think I see in him an intellect profounder and more unique than his contemporaries have yet recognised; because I regard him as the first social regenerator of the day—as the very master of that working corps who would restore to rectitude the warped system of things . . .'

[1] Mrs. Ward's Introduction to the Haworth Edition of *Jane Eyre*: 'The country-house party is equally far from anything known, either to realistic or romantic truth . . .'

Charlotte Brontë's experience of the world was intense but narrow. Of her four books *Villette* and *The Professor* are largely set abroad, while both *Jane Eyre* and *Shirley* are dated in the early years of the century. 'We are going back to the beginning of this century' she says in *Shirley*: 'late years—present years—are dusty, sunburnt, hot, arid. We will evade the noon—forget it in siesta, pass the mid-day in slumber—and dream of dawn.' The narrowness of her experience, her introspection and her small output, all limit the value of her social witness. However, the scene in *Shirley* is relatively wide and extrovert and, both in *Shirley* and *The Professor*, there are references to the North/South theme which was to preoccupy Mrs. Gaskell. Whatever the force of her early Tory inclinations or of her acquired dislike of 'high society', there is a basic honesty of observation and feeling in the greater part of her work which gives it an exceptional authenticity. Jane Eyre was surprised to discover that Mr. Rochester meant to marry 'for interest and connexions' but on reflection did not feel justified 'in judging and blaming either him or Miss Ingram, for acting in conformity to ideas and principles instilled into them, doubtless, from their childhood. All their class held these principles.' Lucy Snowe shows the same coolness of judgement in *Villette*. She makes little account of pedigree and social position herself, but realizes that the world thinks differently and that, to some, 'loss of connection costs loss of self-respect.' 'If a man feels that he would become contemptible in his own eyes, were it generally known that his ancestry were simple and not gentle, poor and not rich, workers and not capitalists, would it be right severely to blame him for keeping these fatal facts out of sight. . . .?'

Shirley must be voicing the mature judgement of her author when she says: 'All ridiculous, irrational crying up of one class, whether the same be aristocrat or democrat . . . is really sickening to me.' In *Jane Eyre* the self-made manufacturer Mr. Oliver is treated kindly, although he could easily have been made to suffer for living in a much grander place than old Mr. Rivers, when his own father had only been a 'journeyman needle-maker'. Jane says of her village scholars: 'I must not forget that these coarsely-clad little peasants are of flesh and blood as good as the scions of gentlest genealogy; and that the germs of native excellence, refinement, intelligence, kind feeling are as likely to exist in their hearts as in those of the best-born.' 'Once and again' (this is from *Villette*) 'I have found that the most cross-grained are by no means the worst of mankind, nor the humblest in station, the least polished in feeling.'

The same lack of prejudice appears in the account of the relations between William Farren, the workman, and the two young ladies in *Shirley*. The middle-aged Mrs. Pryor, who is not at ease with 'the people', 'felt as if a great gulf lay between her caste and his and that to cross it, or meet him half-way, would be to degrade herself.' She finds it difficult to believe that William can have 'fine feelings', though Caroline (and Charlotte) knows perfectly well that he has. Mrs. Pryor's pride—or diffidence—makes her ungenial, and unpopular, with the servants; but it does not lessen Caroline's love or respect for her. No novelist could be more scrupulous in giving Mrs. Pryor, the young ladies and William Farren each their due.

Few observers are so clear-sighted as Charlotte Brontë at her dispassionate best. Had she seen more of the world her work might have lost in concentration of feeling; but, with her fine sense of what was just and honest, she could have outdone her contemporaries in unbiased realism.

* * *

MRS. GASKELL, born Elizabeth Stevenson, was the daughter of a Unitarian minister, who subsequently took up various careers and settled in London. Her mother was descended from an old Lancashire family and died soon after her birth. Elizabeth was brought up modestly, but happily, by an aunt at Knutsford ('Cranford'), was educated for two years at a school in Stratford-on-Avon, and married the Rev. William Gaskell, minister of a Unitarian Chapel in Manchester, when she was 22. Unitarianism appealed to the highly-educated more than most dissenting creeds and Unitarians were socially and culturally to the fore in Manchester; at the same time, as a minister's wife, Mrs. Gaskell was able to learn a good deal about working-class conditions. Apart from Manchester, London, Knutsford and Warwickshire, she had lived in Newcastle-upon-Tyne and had a fondness for Hampshire, where she bought a house shortly before her death. She thus had a much wider knowledge than Charlotte Brontë of English districts and classes.

Sylvia's Lovers is a historical tale, based on a visit to Whitby: Sylvia, a small farmer's daughter, is loved by a Quakerish merchant in the town, but herself falls in love with a dashing seaman who gets press-ganged. The social background is neatly and sympathetically drawn; there are no class conflicts and the gentry make practically no appearance. By contrast *My Lady Ludlow*, which is set in Warwickshire and also goes back to the beginning of the century, portrays—with equal sympathy—a strictly-principled, but tender-hearted and exquisitely courteous *grande dame*, who has very strong views on the duties and privileges of rank. *Ruth*, which was a daring plea for more compassion towards unmarried mothers, describes the seduction of a young girl by a gentleman and her subsequent experience of kindness and unkindness among dissenting people in a Northern town. Apart from the seducer and his mother the characters are chiefly middle class.

But the chief sources of Mrs. Gaskell's inspiration were Knutsford and its neighbourhood, on the one hand, and Manchester on the other. *Cranford* is of course based on the town of Knutsford and evokes tenderly the genteel poverty of its spinster ladies. *Cousin Phillis* also belongs to the Knutsford group: a sad, pastoral, idyll, largely set in the comfortable farmhouse which appears as the home of 'Mr. Thomas Holbrook, yeoman' in *Cranford*. *Wives and Daughters*, Mrs. Gaskell's last book, gives a good sample of rural upper-class and middle-class society in the neighbourhood around Hollingford/Knutsford, dominated by the rather overpowering presence of the Cumnor family. The opening scene is set in 1820 when

'. . . a very pretty amount of feudal feeling still lingered, and showed itself in a number of simple ways, droll enough to look back upon, but serious matters of importance at the time. It was before the passing of the Reform Bill, but a good deal of liberal talk took place occasionally between two or three of the more enlightened freeholders living in Hollingford . . . (nevertheless) every man-jack in the place gave his vote to the liege lord. . . . This was no unusual instance of the influence of the great landowners over humbler neighbours in those days before railways, and it was well for a place where the powerful family, who thus overshadowed it, were of so respectable a character as the Cumnors.'

Manchester, the other pole of her world, was the scene of Mrs. Gaskell's first novel *Mary Barton*. This, like *Ruth*, was written with a social purpose and, except for some rather highly-coloured interiors of the wealthy Carson home, the setting is austerely working-class. *North and South*, a more complex book, relieves Manchester with a few glimpses of Hampshire and London. An impoverished Anglican clergyman, who has lost his faith, arrives in industrial 'Milton' with his well-born wife, her devoted and snobbish maid, and their daughter, and seeks a living by teaching. At the beginning of the book, when the family are still safely in Hampshire, Margaret Hale tells her mother that she is glad they do not visit a coach-building family: 'I don't like shoppy people. I think we are far better off knowing only cottagers and labourers, and people without pretence.' She says that she likes people who have to do with land, the army, the navy and the three learned professions, but not with trade. After arriving in Milton she still dislikes 'the pretence that makes the vulgarity of shop-people'— though the Hales find that their own status is regarded as very dubious there, because they are *not* in trade. However, besides making friends with a working-class family, she gradually learns first to respect, and later to love, the self-made manufacturer Mr. Thornton. As its title suggests—though it was not in fact chosen by Mrs. Gaskell herself—the book contrasts the opposing standards of industry and agriculture, of Manchester and Hampshire, of trade and gentility, and thus attempts a synthesis of the author's personal experience.[1]

Charlotte Brontë touches on one aspect of the North/South conflict in *Shirley*, when the vulgar curate Donne, who laments that 'you scarsley ever see a family where a propa carriage or a

---

[1] Cf. *Mrs. Gaskell* by Edgar Wright (p. 10): 'Mrs. Gaskell was always concerned with how people lived and the social structures that groups of them formed. Her range embraces two extremes, at one end the shifting fabric of society in the industrial England of the times, at the other end the traditional and stratified pattern of social classes which was still the accepted theory, and which existed in the country areas with little impact from industrialisation.'

reg'la butla is kep . . .', abuses Yorkshire for its 'want of high
society . . . the backward state of civilisation . . . the dis-
respectful conduct of the lower orders in the north towards their
betters. . . .' In her *Life of Charlotte Brontë* Mrs. Gaskell notices
the apparent absence of professional middle-class dwellings in the
Yorkshire town of Keighley and says: '. . . nothing can be more
opposed than the state of society, the modes of thinking, the
standards of reference on all points of morality, manners, and even
politics and religion, in such a new manufacturing place as Keighley in the north, and any stately, sleepy, picturesque cathedral
town in the south.' She stresses 'the peculiar force of character
which the Yorkshiremen display', their self-sufficiency, roughness
and resistance to authority, and attributes some of this to their
Norse ancestry. It would seem that, both for her and for Charlotte
Brontë, 'North' and 'South' do not only stand for different ways of
life, for different economic and social systems, but also for different
racial types. Kingsley is another Victorian novelist who felt this
racial contrast.

Mrs. Gaskell admires the rugged Yorkshiremen, though with
some reservations, and she certainly respects the harsh activity of
Manchester, with its sparring masters and men. She makes Margaret Hale tell the working man Higgins, who thinks of going
South: 'You would not bear the dulness of the life; you don't
know what it is; it would eat you away like rust.' Her two 'Manchester' books convey a sense that it is in the North that the battle
lies and the victory must be won. But, if her conscience was in
Manchester, it is clear that her heart was in the 'south'—not indeed
in smart, frivolous, upper-class London (she does not seem to know
the City or the slums) but in the peaceful countrysides of Cheshire,
Warwickshire and Hampshire. The North Pole of Manchester
drew her with its power and worked on her sense of duty;
but it was the South Pole that attracted her and made her feel at
home. She wrote from Oxford in 1857: 'I like dearly to call up
pictures—and thoughts suggested by so utterly different a life to
Manchester. I believe I *am* mediaeval, and *un* Manchester, and *un*
American. I do like Kings and Queens, and nightingales and
mignonettes and roses.'

Nobody could have drawn the gently idealized portrait of Lady
Ludlow unless he had some sympathy with the idea of aristocracy.

Lady Cumnor is certainly rather overwhelming in *Wives and Daughters*; but she is not a bad woman in her grand way and her husband is affability itself. Squire Hamley's family in the same book go back to the Heptarchy ('. . . all those Cumnor people you make such ado of in Hollingford, are mere muck of yesterday . . .') yet 'their mode of life was simple, and more like that of yeomen than squires. Indeed Squire Hamley, by continuing the primitive manners and customs of his fore-fathers, the squires of the eighteenth century, did live more as a yeoman, when such a class existed than as a squire of this generation.' Both the Cumnors and the Hamleys have a sense of obligation towards their dependents and are, by and large, held up for respect.

Like Charlotte Brontë Mrs. Gaskell undoubtedly had a feeling for old family[1]—and it seems in her case to have been unalloyed by Charlotte Brontë's tendency to resent the world of rank and fashion. Similarly she has a kind, if ironical, indulgence for the petty snobberies of Cranford; for the Miss Barkers, for instance, ladies' maids turned milliners, who 'only aped their betters in having "nothing to do" with the class immediately below theirs.' Although Margaret Hale comes to respect Milton, Mrs. Gaskell evidently shares her distaste for the testing of everything 'by the standard of wealth', for the status symbols ('housekeepers, under-gardeners, extent of glass, valuable lace, diamonds, and all such things . . .') vaunted by the women at the Thorntons' dinner party. How far a cry from the 'elegant economy' of Cranford, where:

'. . . it was considered "vulgar" (a tremendous word in Cranford) to give anything expensive, in the way of eatable or drinkable, at the evening entertainments. Wafer bread-and-butter and sponge-biscuits were all that the Honourable Mrs. Jamieson gave; and she was sister-in-law to the late Earl of Glenmire, although she did practise such "elegant economy".'

But, although it is possible to detect some bias in Mrs. Gaskell

---

[1] Cf. the following passage from *Ruth*: '. . . Thurstan was called by his name because my father wished it; for, although he was what people called a radical and a democrat in his ways of talking and thinking, he was very proud in his heart of being descended from some old Sir Thurstan, who figured away in the French wars.'

towards Toryism and gentility, her basic attitude is that of un-prejudiced sympathy with all classes. In all these respects she resembles Charlotte Brontë, though with more experience, less personal antipathy towards grand people, more sentimentality, less unflinching honesty. Two conversations in *Wives and Daughters* illustrate the justice and delicacy of her social perception. In the first the local doctor, Mr. Gibson, is talking to Squire Hamley about young Roger Hamley's desire to marry his stepdaughter (Mr. Gibson, though rumoured to have some good blood, is not a native of the district and is perhaps the nearest thing to a classless man that rural nineteenth-century society could allow):

'I believe her father was grandson of a certain Sir Gerald Kirkpatrick. Her mother tells me it is an old baronetcy. I know nothing of such things.'

'That's something. I do know something of such things, as you are pleased to call them. I like honourable blood.'

'But I'm afraid that only one-eighth of Cynthia's blood is honourable; I know nothing further of her relations excepting the fact that her father was a curate.'

'Professional. That's a step above trade at any rate . . .'

The second conversation is between Molly Gibson and Lady Harriet, one of the Cumnor daughters, who have struck up rather a friendship in spite of their different ages and ranks. Lady Harriet begins by saying of Mr. Preston, the land-agent:

'I cannot bear that sort of person, giving himself airs of gallantry towards one to whom his simple respect is all his duty. I can talk to one of my father's labourers with pleasure, while with a man like that underbred fop I am all over thorns and nettles. . . .'

She goes on to talk of the Miss Brownings:

'I know the Miss Brownings; they used to come regularly on the school-day to the Towers. Pecksy and Flapsy I used to call them. I like the Miss Brownings; one gets enough of respect from them at any rate; and I've always wanted to see the kind of *menage* of such people . . .'

Molly eventually plucks up the courage to say:

'. . . your ladyship keeps speaking of the sort of—the class of people to which I belong as if it was a kind of strange animal you were talking about. . . .'

Lady Harriet replies:

'. . . Don't you see, little one, I talk after my kind, just as you talk after your kind. It's only on the surface with both of us. Why I daresay some of your Hollingford ladies talk of the poor people in a manner which they would consider impertinent in their turn, if they could hear it. But I ought to be more considerate when I remember how often my blood has boiled at the modes of speech and behaviour of one of my aunts, mamma's sister, Lady—No! I won't name names. Any one who earns his livelihood by any exercise of heads and hands, from professional people and rich merchants down to labourers, she calls "persons". She would never in her most slip-slop talk accord them even the conventional title of "gentlemen"; and the way in which she takes possession of human beings, "my woman", "my people",—but, after all, it is only a way of speaking. I ought not to have used it to you; but somehow I separate you from all these Hollingford people . . . most of them are so unnatural in their exaggerated respect and admiration when they come up to the Towers, and put on so much pretence by way of fine manners, that they only make themselves objects of ridicule. You at least are simple and truthful. . . .'

If Mrs. Gaskell placed some value on gentility, she certainly put a much greater one on simplicity and kindness. Though she does not urge drastic change in the social structure, she does plead strongly to humanize it. For all its faults there was more humanity in the traditional system of the countryside than in the relations between masters and men in the manufacturing towns: that was partly why she felt more comfortable in the 'Knutsford' world. But she criticizes no class as such. Even *Mary Barton*, written under an acute sense of the sufferings of the industrial working class, is not intended to attack the manufacturers so much as to awaken their sympathies and win their support for a more humane approach. Afterwards she feared lest it had been too one-sided against the masters, recognizing that to some 'the interests of their work-people are as dear to them as their own'. She tried to strike a fairer balance in *North and South*.

It was not the existence, but the excessive separation of classes that distressed Mrs. Gaskell. This was the message of both her 'Manchester' novels. She says in *Mary Barton*: 'The most deplorable and enduring evil that arose out of the period of commercial depression to which I refer, was this feeling of alienation between the different classes of society'. John Barton's 'overpowering thought, which was to work out his fate on earth, was rich and poor; why are they so separate, so distinct, when God has made them all? It is not His will that their interests are so far apart. Whose doing is it?' Wise Job Legh represents John Barton to Mr. Carson, the manufacturer, not as an 'Owenite' communist or egalitarian, but as hurt by the lack of interest shown in him and his like by the rich:

'It seemed hard to him that a heap of gold should part him and his brother so far asunder. For he was a loving man before he grew mad with seeing such as he was slighted, as if Christ himself had not been poor. At one time, I've heard him say, he felt kindly towards every man, rich or poor, because he thought they were all men alike. But latterly he grew aggravated with the sorrows and suffering that he saw, and which he thought the masters might help if they would.'

North and South preaches the same lesson. Mr. Thornton comes to the conclusion that 'no mere institutions, however wise, and however much thought may have been required to organize and arrange them, can attach class to class as they should be attached, unless the working out of such institutions bring the individuals of the different classes into actual personal contact.'

When, to their delighted confusion, Lady Harriet calls on the Miss Brownings, she behaves as, in her creator's ideal world, everybody would do. For the difficult problem of class division Mrs. Gaskell had a simple, though not an easy solution: that the rich should be genuinely, and uncondescendingly, kind and that the poor should respond to their kindness.

*   *   *

Unlike Mrs. Gaskell, GEORGE ELIOT never attempted a novel of industrial society. This would be surprising in such a 'modern' and serious-minded writer, if it were not that almost all her novels are based on her own early experience of the provincial England of countryside and country town. All her English novels look back to the early 1830s, or earlier, except for her latest, *Daniel Deronda*, which is set in the 1860s. Perhaps most novelists, in their best work, tend to draw on the impressions of society which they formed in their youth, when they were more sensitive to impressions and had more time to absorb them. George Eliot is certainly a striking example of this. When, in *Daniel Deronda*, she tries to portray a new social cluster—the Jews—one feels that she has read a lot about them, but seen comparatively little of their life: the result is that, except for a few pleasant sketches of the Cohen family, the Jewish characters appear as ideas rather than persons. It is very different in her bucolic, pre-Reform, England where the persons are never dwarfed by the author's ideas and are often refreshingly lacking in ideas of their own.

In a sense, then, George Eliot's range is narrower than Mrs. Gaskell's. She certainly made less attempt in her novels to wrestle with contemporary social problems. The circumstances of her life had been different and her genius was more self-centred and profound. She also began writing fiction later. By the sixties—on the whole a curiously quiet decade in English life, though much was happening in the world outside—there was less social unrest and more feeling of security; Mrs. Gaskell herself ceased to grapple with the soot and steam of Manchester.

In another sense, though, George Eliot's world is less limited than that of the two other women novelists. In Charlotte Brontë's novels (though somewhat less so in *Shirley* than the others) we are concerned with a central personality; other people and things appear as part of an individual experience. In Mrs. Gaskell's novels we are continually made aware of a wider world, but we still look at it—as Victorian women would look at it—through the windows of a home. When we read George Eliot we go out into the streets and find ourselves in a full, three-dimensional, world of business and events. In this sense George Eliot is less exclusively a *woman* novelist, though her approach is still feminine enough to ensure a more neutral perception of social relations than the men novelists were usually able, or willing, to achieve.

In so far as Charlotte Brontë had a Tory bias it seems to have been coloured by Anglican principle on the one hand and by a romantic, though controlled, interest in antiquity and gentility on the other. Mrs. Gaskell's Toryism was partly escapist—a nostalgia for a more serene, picturesque and 'mediaeval' world than Manchester—and partly a preference for a social system where the obligations between classes were not solely commercial. If George Eliot shared any Tory leanings it was because of her father, whom she loved and admired, and her early upbringing. At least in her case it was an emotional, rather than an intellectual bias. She wrote late in life: 'Nor can I be sorry, though myself given to meditative if not active innovation, that my father was a Tory. . . . To my father's mind . . . the welfare of the nation lay in a strong Government which could maintain order.'[1] She herself was much influenced by Scott's novels from early childhood. She retained a love of old ways which survived a strong evangelical phase and her later tendency to 'meditative innovation'. She could not have dwelt so much and so kindly on the past without a deep affection for it. Like the two other women novelists she prized its security and, whatever her ideals, she saw a virtue in acceptance as well as revolt.

George Eliot's father, Robert Evans, was born in Staffordshire and brought up as a builder and carpenter. He managed to better himself and did some farming in Derbyshire, before coming to Arbury in 1806 as agent to Francis Newdigate, whose family had been landowners in Warwickshire since the time of Queen Elizabeth. He married a bit above his own birth: Mrs. Evans came of yeoman stock. George Eliot recalls in *Adam Bede* that 'those were times when there was no rigid demarcation of rank between the farmer and the respectable artisan', but nevertheless she makes Mr. Casson say: 'Why Seth's looking rether too high, I should think . . . This woman's kin wouldn't like her to demean herself

[1] Quoted in *George Eliot* by Walter Allen (1964): p. 19.

to a common carpenter.' However, having become agent to a good landed family, Robert Evans was well placed to have dealings with all ranks of country society, from gentry to labourers. He could not have given his daughter a better vantage point for her impressions of provincial life.

Adam Bede is precisely dated in the last years of the eighteenth century and should really count as a historical novel. Its flavour is more exclusively Tory, its social atmosphere more consistently serene, than in the later novels. The whole village of Hayslope is very much under the influence of the Donnithorne family; and the craftsman hero has a more reverential attitude towards his betters than the craftsman hero of *Felix Holt* a generation later. *Mr. Gilfil's Love Story*, from *Scenes of Clerical Life*, goes back to the same period, or earlier. It presents in Sir Christopher Cheverel 'as fine a specimen of the old English gentleman as could well have been found' and, in Mr. Gilfil, an equally fine specimen of the older, rather easy-going, type of Anglican parson. Mr. Gilfil, like Parson Irwine in *Adam Bede*, is popular and a gentleman; George Eliot has an evident fondness for both of them. *Silas Marner*, too, has a distinctly historical flavour, since it goes back to 'the early years of this century'. It describes a village which, unlike Hayslope, has 'no great park and manor-house'; but there are prosperous farmers, or lesser gentry, profiting from the war years when 'the fall of prices had not yet come to carry the race of small squires and yeomen down that road to ruin for which extravagant habits and bad husbandry were plentifully anointing their wheels.'

The Mill on the Floss, Felix Holt the Radical and *Middlemarch* belong to a later period, just before the Reform Bill of 1832. Even this is about a generation before the books were written; but the action falls within George Eliot's own childhood rather than the scope of her father's memories. *The Mill on the Floss* covers a longer passage of time than the two others and is less affected by public events; but a reference to the Duke of Wellington's handling of the Catholic question suggests its date. Socially it revolves around the dead centre of the rural middle class, a world of substantial, and complacent, yeomen and merchants. George Eliot apparently drew on her mother's family to portray the Dodsons, who are majestically satisfied with their own standards and values. Uncle Pullet, who married a Dodson, 'belonged to that extinct class of British yeomen who dressed in good broadcloth, paid high rates and taxes, went to church, and ate a particularly good dinner on Sunday, without dreaming that the British constitution in Church and State had a traceable origin any more than the solar system and the fixed stars. It is melancholy, but true, that Mr. Pullet had the most confused idea of a bishop as a sort of baronet, who might or might not be a clergyman. . . .'

The gentry, let alone the nobility, scarcely impinge on this self-sufficient world. The nearest approach to grandeur is provided when the scene shifts to the local town and we come across the Guests, who owned 'the largest oil-mill and the most extensive wharf in St. Ogg's'. Stephen Guest talks of becoming an M.P. and there is a hint that the Guests may have some connections with the country, since the party at which Stephen kisses Maggie was 'one of the Miss Guests' thoroughly condescending parties, including no member of any aristocracy higher than that of St. Ogg's, and stretching to the extreme limits of commercial and professional gentility.' We are reminded of *Middlemarch*:

'. . . there were nice'distinctions of rank in Middlemarch; and though old manufacturers could not any more than dukes be connected with none but equals, they were conscious of an inherent social superiority which was defined with great nicety in practice, though hardly expressible theoretically.'

Neither the world of St. Ogg's nor the world of the *Floss* countryside is a new world. Society is conservative and old-established families have an advantage. But, if the values are fixed, the level of rank and education is low enough for fortunes and positions to be won and lost. Wealth, reputably earned, confers position; when wealth is lost, position is lost too. There is no titular distinction, no aristocratic mystique, to maintain a condition of genteel poverty. Nor, in most cases, is there enough middle-class refinement to provide a resource, and set a standard, when fortune fails. Maggie herself is an exception. Philip Wakem says of her: 'Miss Tulliver has the only grounds of rank that anything but vulgar folly can suppose to belong to the middle class. She is thoroughly refined, and her friends, whatever else they may be, are respected for irreproachable honour and integrity.' It is significant that he confines this definition to the middle class. He implies that the upper class is set apart by 'rank' and 'blood', the lower class by lack of means and education; the middle class can aspire to distinction but only through wealth (which he despises) or through a combination of culture and integrity.

Felix Holt, which opens with an introduction contrasting the two Englands of rural peace and industrial noise and dirt, is a more complex book and has a wider social range. Although we still do not see much of the labouring class, we meet the gentry, on the one hand, and town-dwelling dissenters, on the other. A rich gallery of middle-class Tories is presented; at the table of the 'Marquis' in Treby 'the many gradations of dignity' range 'from Mr. Wace, the brewer,[1] to the rich butcher from Leek Malton'. There is Mr. Nolan, the former Londoner, who defends trade against the rustic imputation that 'it breeds spindling fellows' and is incompatible with Toryism: 'Plenty of sound Tories have made their fortune by trade. . . . Trade makes property, my good sir, and property is Conservative as they say now.' There is Mr. Scales, the Debarrys' butler, who has not had anything to do with commercial families himself: 'I've those feelings that I look to other things besides lucre. But I can't say that I've not been intimate with parties who have been less nice than I am myself. . . .'

None of this comedy is unsympathetic. Nor are the portraits of the gentry, whether of the Rector of Treby Magna who 'was always of the Debarry family, associated only with county people, and was much respected for his affability'; or of the extremely gentlemanly Philip Debarry who 'treated a servant more deferentially than an equal'; or even of the embittered Mrs. Transome whose 'person was too typical of social distinctions to be passed by with indifference by any one. . . .' We are told, quite kindly, that '. . . genealogies entered into her stock of ideas, and her talk on such subjects was as necessary as the notes of the linnet or the blackbird. She had no ultimate analysis of things that went

[1] Brewing was quite a respectable way of making money, whether on a provincial or national scale. Herbert Pocket tells Pip in *Great Expectations*: 'I don't know why it should be a crack thing to be a brewer; but it is indisputable that while you cannot possibly be genteel and bake, you may be as genteel as never was and brew.'

beyond blood and family. . . . She had never seen behind the canvas with which her life was hung.'

The heroine, Esther, recalls Eppie in *Silas Marner*, whose 'delicate prettiness' was not quite that of a 'common village maiden'. Esther has a native air of breeding which points to the eventual discovery of her gentle birth. She also has a native longing for elegance and refinement, like foolish Hetty in *Adam Bede* to whom 'a gentleman with a white hand was dazzling as an Olympian god', or like Rosamond Vincy in *Middlemarch*, part of whose cleverness was 'to discern very subtly the faintest aroma of rank'. Esther has this cleverness, too. She 'knew quite well that, to Harold Transome, Felix Holt was one of the common people who could come into question in no other than a public light. She had a native capability for discerning that the sense of ranks and degrees has its repulsions corresponding to the repulsions dependent on difference of race and colour. . . .' But she was also of sterner stuff than Rosamond or Hetty; 'she found herself mentally protesting that, whatever Harold might think, there was a light in which he was vulgar compared with Felix. Felix had ideas and motives which she did not believe that Harold could understand.'

For, in spite of its sympathetic treatment of the Tory system and in spite of the basic good feeling which is allowed to permeate class relations, the honours of *Felix Holt* go to its radical hero. It is not indeed easy to define Felix's Radicalism, which is more of an attitude than a creed. But it does emerge that, though he seems to have no precise ideas for reforming the class structure, or even any real wish to overhaul it, his set of values differs from those commonly accepted in the society of his time. In particular he wants to remain a working man and to do something for his fellows; he has no ambition to use his education to climb up the social pole. 'Why should I want to get into the middle class because I have some learning? The most of the middle class are as ignorant as the working people about everything that doesn't belong to their own Brummagen life. That's how the working men are left to foolish devices and keep worsening themselves: the best heads among them forsake their born comrades, and go in for a house with a high door-step and a brass knocker.' Though he does not call for the suppression of the rich, Felix does not approve of their standards. However, his conception of his own place in society has quite a Tory flavour:

'I have my heritage—an order I belong to. I have blood of a line of handcraftsmen in my veins, and I want to stand up for the lot of a handcraftsman as a good lot, in which a man may be better trained to all the best functions of his nature than if he belongs to the grimacing set who have visiting-cards, and are proud to be thought richer than their neighbours. . . . Some men do well to accept riches, but that is not my inward vocation: I have no fellow-feeling with the rich as a class; the habits of their lives are odious to me.'

Middlemarch, which is subtitled 'A study of provincial life', gives the most complete and well-rounded social picture of any of George Eliot's novels; but it does not embrace any new classes or throw much further light on her social attitude. We do however learn more about the relations between the bourgeoisie of a provincial town and the surrounding gentry. Mr. Brooke, who flirts Whiggishly with reform, entertains the professional men of Middlemarch at his country house, for political reasons. The Rector's wife, Mrs. Cadwallader, finds the guests too miscellaneous ('. . . in that part of the country, before Reform had done its notable part in developing the political consciousness, there was a clearer distinction of ranks and a dimmer distinction of parties') and prefers 'the farmers at the tithe-dinner, who drank her health unpretentiously and were not ashamed of their grandfathers' furniture.' But then Mrs. Cadwallader was well-born and had an aristocratic tendency to value the lower more highly than the middle class:

'a lady of immeasurably high birth, descended, as it were, from unknown earls, dim as the crowd of heroic shades—who pleaded poverty, pared down prices, and cut jokes in the most companionable manner, though with a turn of tongue that let you know who she was. Such a lady gave a neighbourliness to both rank and religion, and mitigated the bitterness of uncommuted tithe.'

Even Mr. Brooke, 'always objecting to go too far, would not have chosen that his nieces should meet the daughter of a Middlemarch manufacturer, unless it were on a public occasion.' Men could mix within reason; but ladies must be kept social virgins, so as to tend the flame of class distinction and keep it pure.

Rosamond Vincy is a manufacturer's daughter. One of her hopes in marrying Lydgate is to get 'a little nearer to that celestial condition on earth in which she would have nothing to do with vulgar people, and perhaps at last associate with relatives quite equal to the county people who looked down on the Middle-marchers.' She had once seen 'the Miss Brookes accompanying their uncle at the county assizes, and seated among the aristocracy' and 'had envied them, notwithstanding their plain dress'. Not that the Brookes were deeply aristocratic, but their connections 'were unquestionably "good": if you enquired backward for a generation of two, you would not find any yard-measuring or parcel-tying forefathers—anything lower than an admiral or a clergyman; and there was even an ancestor discernible as a Puritan gentleman who served under Cromwell, but afterwards confor-med, and managed to come out of all political troubles as the proprietor of a respectable family estate.'

In old Mr. Featherstone we catch a last glimpse of the pros-perous yeoman class, living without benefit of gentry, which figures in *Mill on the Floss*. Surveying his funeral Mrs. Cadwallader exclaims to Dorothea Brooke:

'Your rich Lowick farmers are as curious as any buffaloes or bisons, and I daresay you don't half see them at church. They are quite different from your uncle's tenants or Sir James's—monsters —farmers without landlords—one can't tell how to class them.'

George Eliot displays no personal animus against rank; her judgements on all classes are dispassionate and level-headed. (She is less dispassionate when she gets her teeth into pretty, flighty, girls.) What limits or counteracts her Tory nostalgia is the kind of dissenting conscience revealed in *Felix Holt*: an awareness of the fundamental insignificance of social pretensions; a rejection of materialism and an emphasis on other-wordly virtue. But, as she shows in her portrait of Dorothea Brooke, she does not regard such virtue as being incompatible with birth and breeding.

The social scale of *Daniel Deronda* is grander and (except for the

Jews) more restricted than in the earlier novels; although it is much more nearly contemporary, it has less value as a social record. In its excursions into 'Society' the book shows its author's habitual skill at capturing the authentic tone of conversation. Even the terse talk of the aristocratic Grandcourt, the 'heavy swell' who has almost exhausted his capacity for pleasure but still feels an urge to dominate, is impressively convincing. But one misses the provincial accents that enliven the earlier novels. Judaism apart, the book's main purpose is to criticise the Philistinism and artificiality of contemporary English Society, with its tendency to under-value artistic merit and to discourage true feeling. 'How should all the apparatus of heaven and earth . . . make poetry for a mind that has no movements of awe and tenderness. . . . ?' As in *Felix Holt* this seems to be a criticism of the tone, rather than of the structure, of society: an appeal on behalf of deeper and more genuine values. Grandcourt is not condemned as an aristocrat, but as a self-willed martyr to coarse pleasure and tasteless good form.

*   *   *

None of the novels mentioned in this chapter preaches the need for a new social system. Charlotte Brontë may have deplored frivolity or heartlessness in the upper ranks of society; Mrs. Gaskell wanted more humanity in class relations and an improvement in working-class conditions; George Eliot thought that the working class should save itself by its own exertions and would have liked to dethrone the false gods of society's worship. But they all had a certain feeling for traditional social ways and their novels do not urge, or envisage, the growth of an egalitarian society. Were these 'Tory' sympathies (however qualified) typical of female conservatism? Or were they shared by the men novelists?

4. Emphasis

Whatever their purpose in writing fiction, the women novelists took care to describe social relations as they had personally experienced, or honestly imagined, them. The writers discussed in the present chapter of course drew on their own experience, and on honest imagination, too. But, whether deliberately or unconsciously, they exaggerated features of the social system, both for the sake of humour or pathos, and in the hope of stimulating revival or reform.

*   *   *

Though SURTEES paints a brisk and contemporary picture, his scene is rural and his palette pre-Victorian. He is keenly alive to changing habits and fashions in the part of England he sketches; he keeps up, unflaggingly, with the dress of the day and with social behaviour. But his England—sporting, drinking, eating, not too noticeably church-going—seems in essence the England of the Queen's uncles, rather than of her Consort. Industrial strain and religious torment are alike lacking; the moral tone is not particularly elevated; there are no strong lights and darks, but a variety of soiled and cheerful colours.

Except for the famous Mr. Jorrocks—the well-to-do Cockney grocer who lives for sport—Surtees' characters are sharply, but thinly, drawn. His descriptions of fox-hunting are gaily serious; hunting apart, he usually writes for comic effect. The realism achieved by a humorous writer must of course have limits, if only because for most people most of life is not humorous, and because genuine feeling would break the comic spell. Yet anything *can* be taken as a joke and there is usually more realism in comic scenes, however exaggerated, than in false or extravagant serious writing. Comic exaggeration at least implies where the norm should lie. Surtees exaggerates, so as to make people laugh; but his feet are seldom completely off the ground. His method is as he himself describes it in the preface to *Ask Mamma*: 'a mere continuous narrative of an almost every-day exaggeration'. With his flat style, and his curious way of making everything and everybody appear rather, but not impossibly, vulgar, Surtees in fact achieves—at least in his better passages—a robust illusion of a certain kind of life. In surface details, such as dress, the weather, meals, social conversation and travelling arrangements, his accuracy is acute. His concern with important trivia gives his background at least a real authenticity. There is emphasis, certainly, even to the point of caricature; but there is also a solid basis of every-day experience.[1]

Since he was less of a dedicated writer than most Victorian novelists and lived in the world more than in his imagination, Surtees' own background and experience are particularly relevant to his books. He came from an old North country family of apparently unpretentious gentry, his father owning Hamsterley Hall and his maternal uncle sitting in Parliament for South Northumberland. Educated at Durham grammar school he entered a solicitor's office and subsequently took rooms in Lincoln's Inn Fields, before the death of a brother made him his father's heir. Towards the end of his life, in 1856, he became High Sheriff for Durham. He never liked to see his name in print, rejoicing 'in the privilege of writing and printing incognito.' He presumably took to writing in the first place, like Thackeray, as a means of making some money; then he found that it became a habit. In *Mr. Sponge's Sporting Tour* he declares his admiration for 'Mr. Thackeray, who bound up all the home truths in circulation, and many that exist only in the inner chambers of the heart, calling the whole *Vanity Fair* . . .'. But his view of his own productions was modest: 'Writing, we imagine, is something like snuffing or smoking', he says in *Hawbuck Grange*, 'men get into the way of it, and can't well leave it off. Like smoking, it serves to beguile an idle hour.' He was a sportsman and a country gentleman first—and an author afterwards. Perhaps in his attitude to authorship there was not only modesty but a touch of pride—the pride of the gentleman who does not care to become too professional.

Surtees' characters are sometimes placed in London and

[1] Kingsley's comment on *Handley Cross* and *Mr. Sponge's Sporting Tour* (in *Two Years Ago*) is severe but complimentary: '. . . books painfully true to that uglier and baser side of sporting life, which their clever author has chosen so wilfully to portray.'

occasionally in watering places. Once, in *Jorrocks's Jaunts and Jollities*, he makes a trip to Paris. But usually they are to be found in the English countryside, practising—or avoiding—sport. The social range extends from Dukes and other noblemen, through greater and lesser (mostly lesser) gentlemen, doctors, farmers and tradespeople, to horse dealers, grooms and ladies' maids. Urban professional people, clergymen, artists, industrialists and factory workers scarcely appear. There are a good many crooks, but not of the most sinister kind. Almost everybody, whether crooked or not, is faintly seedy and on the make. Noblemen entertain indiscriminately in order to keep up their political interest; most of the gentry pretend to a style of life grander than they can afford; women devote all their efforts to lucrative match-making; horses are sold dishonestly; adventurers and humbugs abound.

Some of Surtees' characters regard money as the only real test of success. Mr. Hazey in *Mr. Romford's Hounds* is of this way of thinking; so is Jerry Pringle in *Ask Mamma* who thinks 'gentility is all very well to talk about, but it gets you nothin' at the market'. But most of them aspire to social distinction as well. The middle ranks of rural society are aflame to 'keep up with the Joneses' and anxious not to be outdone in dressing and dining elegance. Whenever 'company' arrives there is a great flurry of preparation before the visitors are admitted—to find the master and mistress of the house, in rapidly changed clothes, sitting with assumed tranquillity and feigning delighted surprise at the interruption. Everybody notices how many servants everybody else has and what sort of liveries they wear. Young middle-class ladies like the Yammerton girls in *Ask Mamma* are taught nothing sordidly useful, though they can 'play, draw, sing, dance, make wax flowers, bread-stands, do decorative gilding and crochet work.'

The countryside in Surtees' books is not at all a static place socially. It is full of retired tradespeople, or their children, trying to become squires. 'There is nothing a cockney delights in more than aping a country gentleman, and Browne fancied himself no bad hand at it; indeed, since his London occupation was gone, he looked upon himself as a country gentleman in fact.' Jorrocks himself takes Hillingdon Hall and becomes a farming J.P. Sir Moses Mainchance in *Ask Mamma* is great-grandson of Mr. Moses Levy, who dealt in 'complicated penknives, dog-collars and street sponges.' Sir Moses bought a baronetcy, withdrew from commerce and 'set up for a gentleman'. Mr. Large of Pippin Priority in *Mr. Romford's Hounds*, 'was not a sportsman, nor yet a regular Double-imupshire squire, being nothing more or less than a tea-pot-handle maker.' Mr. Marmaduke Muleygrubs, J.P., in *Handley Cross*, had been a stay-maker on Ludgate Hill. But the stays are well buried under Cockolorum Hall, 'a large red-fronted farmhouse, converted by a second owner into a villa; increased by a third into a hall; while under the auspices of its present more aspiring master it was fast assuming the appearance of a castle'; the young Victoria Jemima Muleygrubs is so unaware of the family's past that she is shocked to find Jorrocks a grocer: 'Thell thugar candy! I thought you were a gempleman.'

Puffington in *Mr. Sponge's Sporting Tour* was educated at Eton and Christ Church, but his parents were rich, self-made, business people whose ambition was to make him a gentleman: 'What between the field and college, young Puffington made the acquaintance of several very dashing young sparks—Lord Firebrand, Lord Mudlark, Lord Deuceace, Sir Harry Blueun and others, whom he always spoke of as 'Deuceace,' 'Blueun' etc. in the easy style that marks the perfect gentleman. How proud the old people were of him!' Mrs. Barrington in *Handley Cross*, 'being the daughter of a Leeds manufacturer . . . could not, of course, bear the idea of anything connected with trade.'

In a smaller way the provincial banker Goldspink, in *Plain or Ringlets*, covets a country house, while the Bowderoukins in the same neighbourhood have almost become respectable: 'Bowdey, as the country people called him, had been in the linen line; and Mrs. Roukins's father had been in the flannel trade; but all that was forgotten now, save when they plushed or powdered their footman, set up a dinner bell, or committed any other act of saltation against the peace of their longer retired neighbours' pride and dignity. Then the shop was resuscitated, and the invidious question asked "Who *are* these Bowderoukins's?"'

Most of the satire is easy-going. Surtees does not think any the worse of Jorrocks for becoming a squire; and he seems to have a sneaking admiration for a successful adventurer. But he respects most those who stick to their social last: Tom Scott of Hawbuck Grange, who calls himself 'Mr.' and not 'Esquire'; Mr. Stobb, the rich Yorkshire yeoman or gentleman farmer in *Handley Cross*, who 'clinging to the style of his ancestors, called himself gentleman instead of esquire. . . .' By the same token he despises social pretence. Thus in *Mr. Romford's Hounds*, Independent Jimmy, the local 'bus' driver, ridicules the grandeur of Dalbury Lees, owned by Mr. Watkins who had gone to Australia without any money and come back with it:

'Leuk, noo . . . at them there lodges with the red and gould lion crests and grand fancy gates, just as if they belonged to a duke. Arm dashed but that chap was a painter and glazier, or somethin' of that sort only t'other day. . . .'

Lord Flowerdew's daughters 'speak quite civil and plizant' to Jimmy, but Miss Watkins tells him to get out of the way as if he were a toad: '. . . ar often wonders who those sort o' fondies think they impose upon. It can't be the likes o' me, for we know all about them; it can't be the gentlefolks, for they'll ha' nout to say to them; it mun just be their arn silly sels. . . .'

By contrast Jimmy shortly afterwards exchanges a cordial 'How are you?' with Squire Sterling, whom he respects as a real gentleman, though 'he has neither powdered footmen nor piebald gates'.

Squire Sterling, a sportsman as well as a gentleman, is one of the select few of Surtees' characters who are not only not laughed at, but offered for unqualified approval. They are mostly, if not all, country gentlemen: Mr. Jovey Jessop, in *Plain or Ringlets*; Mr. Neville the M.F.H. in *Hawbuck Grange*, who '. . . sits well into his saddle, and looks like what he is—a gentleman and a sportsman'; the chairman of the St. Boswell cattle show dinner in *Hillingdon Hall*, 'a neighbouring squire of large estate', who 'combined the polished manners of the modern school with the sterling characteristics of the old-fashioned English gentleman. He was at home everywhere, from the palace of the sovereign to the cottage of the labourer. Liberal, high-minded, and gentlemanly, he was looked up to and respected by all.'

None of Surtees' noblemen gets such a good bill. The Dukes of Donkeyton and Tergiversation (with their heirs Lords Bray and Marchhare), Lords Ladythorne and Scamperdale and Lord Lionel

Lazytongs make a rich and pleasantly eccentric collection; but they are all rather ridiculous in one way or another. It is true that, except for the violent Lord Scamperdale, they share with the Duchess of Donkeyton (*Hillingdon Hall*) 'that easy affability and kindness of manner almost invariably the attribute of the high-born';[1] their daughters 'are better calculated for wives, simply because they are generally economically brought up, and are not afraid of losing *caste*, by knowing what every woman ought to do.' But it is clear that Surtees feels more at home with the gentry and that he instinctively looks on the nobility as an exclusive, and even alien, caste.

Mr. Jawleyford of Jawleyford Court, in *Mr. Sponge's Sporting Tour*, though not noble, has the same exotic touch. Although of genuinely old family, he is 'a paper-booted, pen-and-ink' land-owner, who seldom sees his tenants except at tenants' dinners twice a year:

'Then Mr. Jawleyford would shine forth the very impersonifica-tion of what a landlord ought to be. Dressed in the height of the fashion, as if by his clothes to give the lie to his words, he would expatiate on the delights of such meetings of equality . . . he doated on the manly character of the English farmer.'

Mr. Jawleyford has cultivated tastes and is very vain; though he is not given a chance to talk politics, one suspects him of being a Whig.

There is not much sentimentality about Surtees and he is by no means a bigoted *laudator temporis acti*. It is typical of him that, though he finds that railways have destroyed the romance of travelling, he acknowledges that they have improved rural society. The squires have become more independent, less partisan and more widely travelled. In the days before the railways they used to bury themselves on their estates after making the 'Grand Tour'. 'Now they fly about the world, here and there and everywhere, importing ladies from all parts, making the whole kingdom but as

[1] Bill Bowker in *Hillingdon Hall* 'had some breeding in him—by a lord, out of a lady's maid—and blood will tell in men as well as horses. Hence, whatever his difficulties, or whatever his situation, Bill always retained the easy composure of a well-bred man.'

one county . . .' Surtees thinks this is all to the good and that too much energy was devoted to house-building and hospitality in the old days—even though one could be sure of getting excellent port.

Nevertheless there is a hint of conservative nostalgia in Surtees' descriptions of the old Handley Cross neighbourhood ('. . . a rich grazing district full of rural beauties, and renowned for the honest independence of its inhabitants. Neither factory nor foundry disturbed its morals or its quietude—steam and railroads were equally unknown') and of the Heavyside Hunt country, in *Mr. Romford's Hounds*, where there were no factories and people 'seemed happy and contented, more inclined to enjoy what they had than disposed to risk its possession in the pursuit of more. In fact they might be called a three per cent sort of people, in contradistinction to the raving rapacity of modern cupidity.'

Mr. Ballivant, the country lawyer in *Plain or Ringlets*, 'had lived through the rise and growth of the present struggle for station, and did not consider great wealth and happiness altogether synonymous.' A Thackerayan passage in *Mr. Sponge's Sporting Tour*, reflects on the nobility's thirst for wealth: 'Were it not that a "proud aristocracy", as Sir Robert Peel called them, have shown that they can get over any little deficiency of birth if there is sufficiency of cash, we should have thought it necessary to make the best of Mr. Waffles' pedigree, but the tide of opinion evidently setting the other way, we shall just give it as we had it, and let the proud aristocracy reject him if they like. Mr. Waffles' father, then, was either a great grazier or a great brazier. . . .' (In *Ask Mamma*, however, Mrs. Pringle knows that 'though a "proud aristocracy" can condescend, and even worship wealth, yet they are naturally clannish and exclusive and tenacious of pedigree.')

A disapproval of money-grubbing (at least on a grand scale) was an inherited prejudice in Surtees' class and suited his own conservative, if alert, turn of mind. In *Plain or Ringlets* he notes that the squires 'have begun to turn their attention to what their fathers had a great aversion to, namely a little trade, and endeavour to "make both ends meet", as Paul Pry used to say, by a little speculation. . . . We strongly suspect, however, that the squires will find no safer or better speculation than in draining and improving their own land. We do not advocate their teaching the farmers their trade, but we like to see them dispel the prejudices of habit by their example and superior intelligence.'

To judge from his books Surtees was keen on agricultural improvement, so long as it was on practical lines, but contemptuous of theoretical farming. As a landlord, one would suppose him humane but unsentimental. He looks down to tenant farmers as coolly as he looks up to great territorial magnates; there is no contempt for his social inferiors, but there is certainly no idealizing of them. Mr. Ballivant presumably voices his sentiments: 'If gentlemen think to ingratiate themselves with the lower orders by affecting undue familiarity they greatly deceive themselves—the lower orders respect a man in proportion as he respects himself and there is nothing they dislike so much as to see a man who ought to occupy the position of a gentleman demeaning himself by low associates.'

Surtees takes class for granted, thinking that people do better to stick quietly to their station, and delights in ridiculing Mrs. Flather when she plans for her daughter to become Marchioness of Bray. He believes in blood, though he prefers to have it gentle rather than noble. He makes fun out of all kinds of social pretence. But, in spite of this, he is not really a class-conscious writer. The social atmosphere in his books is more relaxed and, in a sense, more democratic than in most Victorian novels. His characters may like being invited to dinner by Dukes, and when they have been, may try and pick up hints for their own entertaining. But, in spite of all the surface snobbery, there is a basic assumption that, in the end, one man is as good as another and that all Englishmen, being free, have the privilege of acting and speaking freely. Jorrocks's cheerful vulgarity triumphs over every obstacle. His maxim is: 'Folks talk about the different grades o' society . . . but arter all's said and done there are but two sorts o' folks i' the world, Peerage folks and Post Hoffice Directory folks. . . .' and, as a Post Office Directory man himself, he has an unabashed way of dealing with the Peerage.

Most of Surtees' principle characters are underbred: Jorrocks himself; Billy Pringle in *Ask Mamma*, who was 'as good an imitation of a swell as ever we saw' and had 'all the airy dreaminess of an hereditary highflyer' but was, after all, the son of a former lady's maid; the smooth sporting adventurer Sponge; the rough sporting adventurer Romford (offspring of a gardener and another lady's maid) who found it useful to be taken for a landed gentleman of the same name. Except perhaps for Billy—who was no sportsman—Surtees is at home with all of them and treats them with the cool affection which is the nearest he gets to warmth.

It is of course easier to make underbred heroes amusing—and indeed Mr. Bunting, the less underbred hero of *Plain or Ringlets*, fails to make any impression at all. But a number of passages, paticularly in the early *Jorrocks's Jaunts and Jollities*, suggest that Surtees rather relished raffishness and vulgarity and that his friends, when he was a young man in London, were not necessarily of the politest or most respectable kind. A public school, followed by Oxford or Cambridge, would presumably have given his education more of a class bias than Durham Grammar School. Then again life in the rural South was more graded and deferential than in the rougher North. In Surtees' countryside there is a sense both of independence and of interdependence, which gives a bluntness and directness to social relations.

But the chief levelling influence in Surtees' writings is, of course, sport. '"But see"' cries Mr. Jorrocks at Newmarket, '"Lord —— is talking to the Cracksman." "To be sure," replies Sam, "that's the beauty of the turf. The lord and the leg are reduced to an equality. Take my word for it, if you have a turn for good society, you should come upon the turf——."' What is true of the turf is true of the hunting field. Surtees' hunts are never very fashionable or exclusive and his fields are a motley social lot; but his sportsmen have a regard for each other, whatever their social status. It is as a hunting man that Tom Scott is invited to stay by Lord Lionel Lazytongs, while Romford is forgiven everything because he really knows how to hunt. The fox-hounds are of course socially a cut above the harriers (Mr. Jovey Jessop is a gentleman, while Mr. Jonathan Jobling is not); but even between fox-hunter and harrier there is a sporting equality and a basis for mutual respect.

Sport being what Surtees most cared about—at least as a writer—the sporting standard becomes the most important in his work. Other things—farming, conversation, journeys, food and drink—have their place because they make sport possible or attractive. Class, taste, love, even morality, occupy the background, looking much less important than they normally do in Victorian novels. As a result, for all the accuracy of his social observation and the comic emphasis of his social descriptions, Surtees comes nearer to a classless approach than any other writer in this book.

*　　*　　*

Many people find DICKENS's characters and descriptions exaggerated; others see them as dreadfully true to life. But nobody can deny that he is an emphatic writer. He is emphatic like Surtees through wanting to make people laugh, particularly in *Pickwick Papers*, his first book, which owed a good deal to *Jorrocks's Jaunts and Jollities*. At other times he is emphatic because he wants to make people cry. He is also emphatic, like Disraeli and Kingsley but more powerfully than either, in his eagerness to highlight and correct abuses. But all of this seems to come from an inner emphasis in his imagination, which demanded clear outlines and strong lights and colours and was apt to picture the weather as remarkably hot, remarkably delightful, remarkably foggy or remarkably stormy.

As his Prefaces to *Martin Chuzzlewit* and *Dombey and Son* show, Dickens was eager to vindicate the correctness of his reading of character; he often goes out of his way to claim accuracy for accounts of social and other phenomena that his critics might consider overdone. He aimed at truth—and indeed there is little, even in his most bizarre characters, that is psychologically impossible; more often their behaviour reveals an extraordinary insight into human motives and instincts. Nor are most of his scenes, however dramatic, absolutely improbable in themselves. What makes his work seem exaggerated and—when the novelist's spell is broken—suspends belief, is his frequent portrayal of a general state of affairs by an extreme instance and the way in which his characters parade essential qualities in unalloyed gloss. In each case it is the vividness and, in a sense, the simplicity of Dickens's imagination that produces this effect. His characters are capable of growth and change (young Martin Chuzzlewit and Bella Wilfer in *Our Mutual Friend* both change conspicuously for the better); but, at any given time, they exemplify some particular

characteristic, virtue, or vice. Little in Dickens is muted or qualified: while this heightens the power and brilliance of his treatment,
it tends to remove his world from the world of half-lights and
mixed feelings that most of us know. The effect is, to some extent,
unreal, but because of an excess of reality. Similarly his characters
often show their thoughts or natures by their speech in a way that
seems artificial, because it is too articulate and too little softened or
distorted by social conventions.

A particular instance is the way in which some of Dickens's
rich, grand, people address the poor. Although Victorians were
quite clear who their social inferiors were, and were a good deal
les inhibited from using a *de haut en bas* style of speaking to them
than seems possible today, they can seldom have been quite so
offensive and arrogant as Dickens makes them out to have been.
It was never gentlemanly to be gratuitously offensive to social
inferiors, though there was no doubt a fair amount of patronising,
even among the gentlemanly. Allan Woodcourt in *Bleak House* is
commended for his habit, in speaking to the poor, of 'avoiding
patronage or condescension, or childishness (which is the favourite
device, many people deeming it quite a subtlety to talk to them like
little spelling books)'. There is a good deal of such condescension
in Victorian novels; but nobody depicts social arrogance so
frequently and so poignantly as Dickens. The offensive expressions
which he puts in the mouths of some of his characters become a
little easier to accept when they are read not so much as actual
speech (which ordinary social usage must have toned down) but as
reproducing, with dramatic emphasis, an inner habit of indifference
or disdain.

The purity and simplicity of Dickens's feelings is shown
throughout his work in an extreme sensitivity to arrogance and
condescension of any kind. He attacks insular British complacency
whether in the working class Bleeding Hearts' Yard of *Little
Dorrit* or in the stuffy conversation of the businessman Podsnap
in *Our Mutual Friend*. He knows of course that snobbery is an
engrained English characteristic. Observing Tony Weevle's
pictures of society beauties Mr. Tulkinghorn, in *Bleak House*, notes
that he takes 'a strong interest in the fashionable great . . . a
virtue in which few Englishmen are deficient'. At the Waterbrooks'
dinner party in *David Copperfield* 'the conversation was about the

Aristocracy—and Blood. Mrs. Waterbrook repeatedly told us, that if she had a weakness, it was Blood'. Another lady at the dinner regarded Blood as something tangible, which admitted of no doubt, unlike 'services, intellect, and so on. . . .': 'We see Blood in a nose and we know it. We meet with it in a chin, and we say, "There it is! That's Blood!".' Dickens can be tolerant of harmless snobbery like that of the worthy Mr. Meagles in *Little Dorrit*. He can understand, perhaps even sympathise with, Emily's wish to become a lady in *David Copperfield*, or Pip's wish to become a gentleman in *Great Expectations*. But the central theme of *Great Expectations* is the wrongness, or at least the folly, of this ambition.

True feeling (Dickens would have us conclude) is to be found more easily in the lower, than in the upper, ranks of society. It is a part of Steerforth's egotism, in *David Copperfield*, that he cannot see this. When Miss Dartle asks him:

'That sort of people. Are they really animals and clods, and beings of another order? I want to know *so* much.'

he replies:

'Why, there's a pretty wide separation between them and us . . . They are not to be expected to be as sensitive as we are. Their delicacy is not to be shocked, or hurt very easily. They are wonderfully virtuous, I dare say. . . .'

For Dickens there was more true feeling among the poor, except when brutalized by oppression or extreme poverty, because they had been less intellectualized and less exposed to the corruption of an acquisitive civilization. It was a central part of his creed to believe in the natural goodness and innocence of ordinary people. Where things went wrong in society it was less because of basic weaknesses in human character, or because of conflicts between honestly irreconcilable interests or ideals, than because, through some malignant agency, the stream of life had been deflected from its proper course. The fault must lie with those in power. Distortions caused by oppression would seek correction in revolution before natural peace and prosperity could recur. Thus in *A Tale of Two Cities* he writes of the French Revolution and the *ancien régime*:

'Crush humanity out of shape once more, under similar hammers, and it will twist itself into the same tortured forms. Sow the same seed of rapacious licence and oppression over again, and it will surely yield the same fruit according to its kind.'

There must be some personal explanation for this emotional bias of Dickens's: something in his own temperament or upbringing which had implanted a bright belief in essential goodness and happiness, together with a dark sense of the heartless forces prone to distort them. Possibly there is a key in the happiness of his early, and the misery of his later, childhood. Whatever its origin, it was this bias—so opposed to a Conservative's obsession with original human weakness—that lay behind his hatred of government and developed the radical principles in which (he wrote in 1841[1]) he waxed stronger every day. Shortly before his death he said: 'My faith in the people governing is, on the whole, infinitesimal; my faith in the People governed is, on the whole, illimitable'; and again: '. . . law-givers are nearly always the obstructors of society instead of its helpers . . . in the extremely few cases where their measures have turned out well, their success has been owing to the fact that, contrary to their usual custom, they have implicitly obeyed the spirit of their time, and have been —as they always should be—the mere servants of the people. . . .'[2]

Anything institutional or official was bound to grate on Dickens, if only because of its impersonal character. For Scrooge's nephew in *A Christmas Carol* the great virtue of Christmas was that it induced men and women 'to think of people below them as if they really were fellow-passengers to the grave, and not another race of creatures bound on other journeys.' It is not surprising that Dickens deeply distrusted the whole machinery of government and the law. Politicians, officials and—with a few honourable exceptions—lawyers are his bugbears, together with professional philanthropists and agitators: in fact any impersonal or patronizing assumption of authority was distasteful to him. By contrast doctors and clergymen (like Mr. Milvey in *Our Mutual Friend* and Mr. Crisparkle in *Edwin Drood*), who work to relieve individual suffering, have his warm approval. So do seafaring people, whose innocence has escaped the corruption of dry land. In one passage

[1] Quoted in Edgar Johnson's *Charles Dickens his tragedy and triumph*.
[2] Quoted by Edgar Johnson: op. cit.

in *Dombey and Son* there is a contrast between the unsympathetic magistrate or judge admonishing 'the unnatural outcasts of society' and 'the good clergyman or doctor, who, with his life imperilled at every breath he draws, goes down into their dens. . . .'

Dickens's first two novels, *Pickwick Papers* and *Oliver Twist*, while already exposing abuses, are free from class feeling. The relationship between classes in *Pickwick Papers* is good-humoured, though there is a passing reference to the fierce Captain Boldwig, whose wife's sister had married a marquis and whose 'house was a villa, and his land "grounds", and it was all very high, and mighty, and great.' In *Oliver Twist* the better characters are drawn from the upper ranks of society, while individual villainy is to blame for the worst of Oliver's sufferings.

In the following books (*Nicholas Nickleby, Old Curiosity Shop* and *Martin Chuzzlewit*) the emphasis is still on individual villains and particular abuses. But a number of passages suggest a growing preoccupation with the arrogance of 'superior' people. Mr. Gregsbury, the M.P. in *Nicholas Nickleby*, refers to 'the natural care of not allowing inferior people to be as well off as ourselves—else where are our privileges?' When rich customers are rude to Kate Nickleby in Madame Mantalini's shop Dickens is stung to exclaim: 'May not the complaint, that common people are above their station, often take its rise in the fact of *un*common people being below theirs?' In *Old Curiosity Shop* Miss Monflathers, surrounded by her ladies' seminary, tells Nell how naughty she is to be a wax-work child when she could be working in a factory:

' "The little busy bee" said Miss Monflathers, drawing herself up, "is applicable only to genteel children,
In books or work or healthful play
is quite right as far as they are concerned; and the work means painting on velvet, fancy needlework, or embroidery. In such cases as these", pointing to Nell, with her parasol, "and in the case of all poor people's children, we should read it thus—
In work, work, work. In work alway let my first years be past, that I may give for ev'ry day some good account at last." '

The next two books, *Dombey and Son* and *David Copperfield*, have their villains, too; but these bulk less large and there is more stress on the environment which formed them. Mr. Dombey himself, though not quite a villain, is devilishly proud:

'Was Mr. Dombey's vice, that ruled him so inexorably, an un-natural characteristic? It might be worth while, sometime, to inquire what Nature is, and how men work to change her, and whether, in the enforced distortions so produced, it is not natural to be unnatural. Coop any son or daughter of our mighty mother within narrow range, and bind the prisoner to one idea, and foster it by servile worship of it on the part of the few timid or designing people standing round, and what is nature to the willing captive who has never risen up upon the wings of a free mind—drooping and useless soon—to see her in her comprehensive truth?'

In the same book the blighting effects of bad education are seen both in the death of little Paul Dombey, who has been expensively forced, and in the way in which Rob Toodle goes to the bad after a heartless education at a charitable institution. Mr. Dombey explains why he has procured Rob's admittance there:—

'I am far from being friendly to what is called by persons of levelling sentiments, general education. But it is necessary that the inferior classes should continue to be taught to know their position, and to conduct themselves properly. So far I approve of schools.'

David Copperfield was himself lucky enough to finish his schooling under a good schoolmaster; but Uriah Heep's false humility had been dinned into him at a foundation school which 'taught us all a deal of umbleness'.

The importance of education, in Dickens's scheme of things, was of course capital. As bad education could blight, so good education could release and develop the natural faculties for good. He told the Leeds Mechanics' Institute that popular education would 'end in sweet accord and harmony among all classes. . . .' His dream, in *Dombey and Son*, was of the day when men 'delayed no more by stumbling-blocks, of their own making' would 'apply themselves, like creatures of one common origin, owing one duty to the Father of one family, and tending to one common end, to make the world a better place!'

Emphasis

Among Dickens's later books *A Tale of Two Cities* and *Great Expectations* stand together, and apart, as two shorter novels, written with great power and verve, having less richness of character and more sweep of plot than is usual in his work, each depending on a single, closely-knit, theme. Yet even these two books illustrate the shift in Dickens's interest, as he grew older, from the evil influence of individuals to that of environments. (*Edwin Drood*, his last novel, suggests a reversion to the earlier type; but the book is too incomplete for Jasper's villainy to be fully explored and explained.) *A Tale of Two Cities* is of course a story of individuals, but of individuals absorbed into a background drama of oppression and revolution. *Great Expectations* is the story of an individual, but one caught in a conflict between two different social settings.

The remaining books, rich and complex in Dickens's usual manner, develop the abuses of the earlier novels to the point where these abuses themselves become the villains of the piece. They are no longer attacked in digressions, or figure as part of a chain of incidents. The harm that they do is central to the story; their blighting, or corrupting, influence is felt throughout. Thus the villains of *Bleak House* are the Court of Chancery and oppressive, impersonal, philanthropy. *Hard Times*, written after a visit to Preston, attacks the inhumanity of industrial society, the bleak teachings of political economy and the aridity of purely factual education. *Little Dorrit* satirizes the ascendancy of speculative wealth over society, and hits hard at the obstructive bureaucracy of the Circumlocution Office, presided over by the well-born Barnacles, with their one, negative, skill of 'How not to do it'. *Our Mutual Friend*, besides illustrating the failures of the Poor Law in Betty Higsden's fear of the Workhouse, shows up the heartlessness and hollowness of the artificial social circle collected by the rootless Veneerings, with their old friends (who are in fact all new), their table decorations of silver camels and their eventual collapse into bankruptcy.

Mr. Veneering becomes an M.P.; but his dinners are only on the verge of fashion. Old Mr. Twemlow, the second cousin of a peer, is about the best he can do, together with Lady Tippins, the relict of a man who had been knighted by mistake by George III. There are grander dinners in *Little Dorrit*, given by Mr. Merdle, the financial swindler. *Little Dorrit* also provides a glimpse of genuinely aristocratic society in the persons of the Barnacles and their allies, the Stiltstalkings. Mrs. Gowan, born into this society, collects a small party in her Grace and Favour appartment at Hampton Court; this sets the scene for a brilliant little skit of 'Inner Circle' talk. Mrs. Gowan thinks that, 'if John Barnacle had but abandoned his most unfortunate idea of conciliating the mob' all would have been well and the country preserved. Another lady thinks Augustus Stiltstalking should have ordered the cavalry out. Somebody else thinks the newspapers should have been muzzled:

'It was agreed that the country (another word for the Barnacles and Stiltstalkings) wanted preserving, but how it came to want preserving was not so clear. It was only clear that the question was all about John Barnacle, Augustus Stiltstalking, William Barnacle and Tudor Stiltstalking, Tom, Dick, or Harry Barnacle or Stilt-stalking, because there was nobody else but mob. And this was the feature which impressed Clennam, as a man not used to it, very disagreeably: making him doubt if it were quite right to sit there, silently, hearing a great nation narrowed to such little bounds.'

Mrs. Gowan courts Mrs. Merdle and does her best to spread the totally false idea that her son has been entrapped into marriage by the middle-class Meagles family. None of this is very endearing. The picture of aristocratic society in *Bleak House*, though critical, is more sympathetically, or at least more carefully, so. The 'world of fashion' is presented as restricted to a five-mile radius, yet thinking it controls everything: '. . . a very little speck. There is much good in it; there are many good and true people in it; and it has its appointed place. But . . . a deadened world, and its growth is sometimes unhealthy for want of air.' Like the Court of Chancery it is a thing of 'precedent and usage'; both are 'over-sleeping Rip Van Winkles, who have played at strange games through a deal of thundery weather'.

At Chesney Wold, the country seat of Sir Leicester Dedlock, Baronet:

'The brilliant and distinguished circle comprehends within it no contracted amount of education, sense, courage, honour, beauty and virtue. Yet there is something a little wrong about it, in despite of its immense advantages. What can it be?'

Dickens's answer is a kind of spiritual Dandyism, a determination to put the clock back or to 'put a smooth glaze on the world, and to keep down all its realities', an insistence on treating politics as a family affair.

Dickens was not totally antipathetic to aristocrats as such. He was always ready to have a fling at empty-headed young peers like Lord Mutanhed in *Pickwick Papers* and Lord Frederick Verisopht in *Nicholas Nickleby*, or at well-connected cynics like Harthouse in *Hard Times* and Gowan in *Little Dorrit*. But his own experience of the world, and of society, made him aware that there were heads and hearts in the upper class, however much he might resent its pride and self-absorption. He had a soft spot for 'the best and brightest of the Barnacles' in *Little Dorrit*, for the kindly Lord Feenix in *Dombey and Son* and for the dry, honourable, Twemlow in *Our Mutual Friend*. His fullest-length portrait of an aristocrat is of Sir Leicester Dedlock in *Bleak House*—a stiff, but not an essentially unfair, likeness. The Dedlocks had always been arrogant, conventional and lacking in talent; but they were also men of honour. Sir Leicester, who admits Nature to be a good idea though 'an idea dependent for its execution on your great county families', is 'an honourable, obstinate, truthful, high-spirited, intensely prejudiced, perfectly unreasonable man'. Although determined that nobody should ever encourage 'some person in the lower classes to rise up somewhere—like Wat Tyler', he is 'an excellent master'. His devotion to his wife is touching and gallant and he is kind and generous 'according to his dignified way' to his poor relations, the major part of whom are 'amiable and sensible, and likely to have done well enough in life if they could have overcome their cousinship.'

In spite of a touch of exaggeration, one of the most effective scenes in *Bleak House*—offering a kind of North/South contrast which extends even 'to the strong Saxon face of the visitor'—occurs between Sir Leicester and the younger son of his housekeeper, Mr. Rouncewell, a self-made industrialist. Mr. Rouncewell's son has fallen in love with a village girl who has won Lady

Dedlock's favour and become her maid. Mr. Rouncewell, who has educated his own children to take a higher place in society, tells Sir Leicester that, though 'unequal marriages' are not uncommon in his class between sons of industrialists and factory girls, he would like to arrange for his prospective daughter-in-law to receive some education herself before she marries his son. Sir Leicester feels that the floodgates are being opened and that the girl cannot possibly do better than to remain with his wife. He says, stiffly: 'Mr. Rouncewell, our views of duty, and our views of station, and our views of education, and our views of—in short all our views—are so diametrically opposed that to prolong this discussion must be repellent to your feelings and repellent to my own'. Nevertheless, arrogant and narrow-minded as he is, it is 'with all the nature of a gentleman shining in him' that he concludes by saying that it is late and dark and by urging Mr. Rouncewell to stay the night.

This scene, with its clash between enterprise and feudal duty, contrasts aristocracy and capitalism. In *Hard Times* there is a kind of alliance between them. Similarly, while the City does not mix with the West End at Mr. Dombey's dinner party, there is a kind of collusion between the worlds of fashion and finance in *Little Dorrit* and *Our Mutual Friend*. In these later books there is a more general onslaught on the powers that be and those who are ambitious to join them. There is little sympathy for Charley Hexam, in *Our Mutual Friend*, in his selfish struggle to raise himself in the scale of society. Mr. Rouncewell deserves respect and the success his efforts have won him; but Mr. Bounderby, in *Hard Times*, is a man 'who could never sufficiently vaunt himself a self-made man. A man who was always proclaiming, through that brassy-speaking-trumpet of a voice of his, his old ignorance and his old poverty. A man who was the Bully of humility'.

Many, perhaps most, of the best people in Dickens's novels are drawn from the lower class: the Nubbles family in *Old Curiosity Shop*, the Toodle family in *Dombey and Son*, the Peggottys in *David Copperfield*, Joe Gargery in *Great Expectations*, Mr. and Mrs. Boffin in *Our Mutual Friend*. They all overflow with the warmth of heart and the true feeling that Dickens cherished. When the guilty Mrs. Lammle felt ashamed under Georgiana Podsnap's embrace, both the Boffins 'understood her instantly, with a more delicate subtlety than much better educated people, whose perception came less directly from the heart, could have brought it to bear upon the case'. The Nubbles household is poor but loving:

'. . . if ever household affections and loves are graceful things, they are graceful in the poor. The ties that bind the wealthy and the proud to home may be forged on earth, but those which link the poor man to his humble hearth are of the truer metal and bear the stamp of Heaven. The man of high descent may love the halls and lands of his inheritance as a part of himself: as trophies of his birth and power; his associations with them are associations of pride and wealth and triumph; the poor man's attachment to the tenements he holds, which strangers have held before, and may tomorrow occupy again, has a worthier root, struck deep into a purer soil.'

But there are worthy middle-class characters in Dickens's novels, too. His radicalism was not doctrinaire; he found no fault with an honest *bourgeois* way of life. Particular abuses apart, it was not so much a change of system, as a change of heart and attitude, that he preached. He saw nothing degrading in domestic service (witness Sam Weller and Mark Tapley) or in decent business (witness the Cheeryble brothers and Doyce and Clennam) or even in inherited wealth (witness Dick Swiveller, John Westlock and John Harmon). Although strongly against a calculating, materialist attitude, whether in business or in private life, he could recognize something frigidly honourable in a big business House like Dombey and Son or Tellsons in *A Tale of Two Cities*. At the end of *Dombey and Son* the young hero, Walter Gay, is left with the prospect of building up an equally, or even more, famous firm. In *Our Mutual Friend* John Harmon says to his wife: '. . . all people are not the worse for riches, my own. . . . Not even most people, it may be hoped. If you were rich, for instance, you would have a great power of doing good to others.'

The portrait of Sir Leicester Dedlock is not an unfair one, but he never fully comes alive, and it is only after he has had a stroke that he becomes really convincing. Most of Dickens's upper-class characters are relatively colourless, while his working-class characters, when good at all, tend to be too good for this world. It is in the portrayal of people from the lower half of the middle class that he excels; they may be larger than life but they are wholly and wonderfully alive. This was of course the *milieu* in which Dickens was brought up himself. His father, who had a post in the Navy Pay Office, struggled after gentility but was always in money difficulties. His grandparents had been steward and housekeeper at Crewe Hall (Mrs. Rouncewell of Chesney Wold is presumably a tribute to them). He himself, after a chequered education, became a solicitor's clerk at the age of 15.

Dickens assumed the right to use the crest of an old Staffordshire family of the same name, with which his own may once have been connected. His radicalism did not prevent him from this much interest in gentility; nor did it stop him sending his eldest son to Eton, or regretting the absence of 'humanising conventionalities' in the United States. Several quotations from his work would show that, no less than other Victorian novelists, he was preoccupied by 'gentlemanly' standards. Besides Cousin Feenix and Mr. Twemlow he produces a number of sympathetic gentlefolk: Mr. Wardle in *Pickwick Papers*,[1] the Maylies in *Oliver Twist*, Mr. Jarndyce in *Bleak House* ('such a true gentleman in his manner, so chivalrously polite'). Oliver Twist himself justifies his extraordinary delicacy of feeling by turning out to be the illegitimate son of a gentleman with wealthy and important connections, by the daughter of a retired naval officer. Little Nell in *Old Curiosity Shop* is (like Little Dorrit) of good family: Mrs. Jarley, the wax-work proprietress for whom she had worked, had always said it: 'I knew she was not a common child'. Nicholas Nickleby regards himself as a gentleman's son. The poor Smike, whom he befriends, turns out to be his cousin, though only after a revealing sneer by Ralph Nickleby, who presents him fraudulently to Nicholas as Mr. Snawley's son:

'Your romance, sir, is destroyed, I take it. No unknown; no persecuted descendent of a man of high degree; the weak imbecile son of a poor petty tradesman. We shall see how your sympathy melts before plain matter of fact'.

[1] Mr. Wardle's style of life is perhaps less that of a gentleman than that of a substantial yeoman of the old type. But his mother's family 'came over with Julius Caesar' and had a member beheaded by 'a Henry'.

But the romantic appeal of gentility is more noticeable in the early novels. Later on, although the ambiguity in the terms 'lady' and 'gentleman' is never resolved, gentlemanliness tends to become a characteristic found in all classes, wherever there is truth, gentleness and honour. When Pip tells Biddy, in *Great Expectations*, that he plans to become a gentleman, she does not think it would answer and says: '. . . don't you think you are happier as you are?' In the end it does, in a way, answer, but only after Pip has realized the falsity of his ambition and accepted that there could be nothing better than the unassuming kindness of Joe and Biddy. Even in the earlier novels gentility of birth and behaviour is not a predominant theme. Moved by the active generosity of the self-made Cheeryble brothers[1] Nicholas Nickleby exclaims: 'Good Lord! and there are scores of people of their own station, knowing all this and twenty times more, who wouldn't ask these men to dinner because they eat with their knives and never went to school!' *Martin Chuzzlewit* opens with a satirical skit on the pedigree of the Chuzzlewit family:

'As no lady or gentleman, with any claims to polite breeding, can possibly sympathise with the Chuzzlewit Family without being first assured of the extreme antiquity of the race . . .'

Dickens never fully succumbed to the lure of the past. He was the least nostalgic of Victorian novelists. In his pictures of the late eighteenth century, in *Barnaby Rudge* and *A Tale of Two Cities*, he goes out of his way to emphasize the inconvenience and brutality of the times. In *The Chimes* he satirizes backward-looking Toryism in the person of a red-faced, past-loving, gentleman in a blue coat.

' "The good old times, the grand old times, the great old times! *Those* were the times for a bold peasantry, and all that sort of thing. Those were the times for every sort of thing in fact. There's nothing now-a-days. Ah!" sighed the red-faced gentleman, "The good old times, the good old times!"

'The gentleman didn't specify what particular times he alluded

[1] Based on the Grant brothers of Manchester, with whom Dickens had dined.

to; nor did he say whether he objected to the present times, from disinterested consciousness that they had done nothing very remarkable in producing himself.'

Like other Victorian novelists Dickens was highly critical of marriages based on interest, not love. In *Oliver Twist* there is a reference to '. . . the wretched marriage, into which family pride, and the most sordid and narrowest of all ambition' forced Oliver's father 'when a mere boy'. The heartless Lammle marriage in *Our Mutual Friend*, and the heartless Bounderby marriage in *Hard Times*, are exploited to the full. So is Mr. Dombey's second marriage, in *Dombey and Son*, where the mercenary match-making of his mother-in-law is paralleled, at a much lower level of society, by the pandering of Mrs. Brown:

'In this round world of many circles within circles, do we make a weary journey from the high grade to the low, to find at last that they lie close together, that the two extremes touch, and that our journey's end is but our starting-place?'

This is a fairly conventional Victorian reaction to what was, nevertheless, quite conventional Victorian practice. Where Dickens goes further than most of his contemporaries is in his readiness to envisage marriage between widely different social classes. Mr. Toots in *Dombey and Son*, who has inherited independent means, marries the former nursemaid, Susan Nipper: admittedly he is weak-minded, but the most sensible thing he does is to marry her. Pip in *Great Expectations* is only a gentleman by education, but perhaps all the more conscious of his acquired status; yet he comes to the conclusion that he ought to marry Biddy and it is only because she has already decided to marry Joe Gargery that he is left free for the glamorous Estella. In *Our Mutual Friend* Eugene Wrayburn, a gentleman, marries Lizzie Hexam, a waterman's daughter. He has already given her some education; he is not hampered by interfering relations; she is beautiful and she has saved his life. All this of course makes the thing easier. Even before she saved his life he told his friend, Mortimer Lightwood: 'There is not a better girl in all this London . . . no better among my people at home; no better among your people'. Nevertheless society (or at least the circle of the Veneerings) does not approve of the marriage, and Dickens has to put up old Mr. Twemlow to defend it:

'If this gentleman's feelings of gratitude, of respect, of admiration, and affection, induced him . . . to marry this lady, I think he is a greater gentleman for the action, and makes her the greater lady. I beg to say, that when I use the word, gentleman, I use it in the sense in which the degree may be attained by any man. The feelings of a gentleman I hold sacred, and I confess I am not comfortable when they are made the subject of sport or general discussion.'

Dickens's last completed novel closes on this note. It is left to a gentleman by birth to insist that true gentlemanliness does not depend on birth or position. Whatever the verdict of society, Eugene Wrayburn's human feeling triumphs over class at the point where class differences are most difficult to bridge. The symbolic importance of the triumph is great. But there is no repudiation of gentlemanly standards.

* * *

DISRAELI's emphasis is rarely comic; his best comic effects were achieved by a grave and disciplined use of wit. It is in his most serious moods that the theatrical splendour of his imagination luxuriates. His heroes may or may not be overdrawn; but the backcloths to their lives are regularly painted with dramatic intensity. At his most restrained he relishes the grand and romantic. At his less restrained he loves to dazzle with transformation scenes where the lights turn from rose-pink, through fiery red, to caerulean blue.

In a scathing passage in his *Autobiography* Trollope wrote of Disraeli's effect on the young: 'He has struck them with astonishment and aroused in their imagination ideas of a world more glorious, more rich, more witty, more enterprising, than their own. But the glory has ever been the glory of pasteboard, and the wealth has been a wealth of tinsel. The wit has been the wit of hair-

dressers, and the enterprise has been the enterprise of mounte-
banks. . . . Through it all there is a feeling of stage properties,
a smell of hair-oil, an aspect of buhl, a remembrance of tailors, and
that pricking of the conscience which must be the general accom-
paniment of paste diamonds.'

Disraeli's dramatic emphasis is particularly striking in his pictures of 'society': in his shots of stately homes and fashionable
parties. Everything, even the boredom, is colourful and amusing.
Everybody looks good or distinguished; the *décor* impresses or
captivates; the flattest talk has an epigrammatic quality. Yet, in
spite of all the gloss, Disraeli's accounts of 'society' are more
authentic than those of the other Victorian novelists discussed in
this book. He was the only one to feel really at home in the great
world. He had seen a good deal of it when still a young man. By
the end of his life it had become his own circle.

Perhaps this was because, although not born in the world of
'society', Disraeli never fully belonged to any other circle. His
own temperament and background had made him something of an
outsider from the start; he was free to find his own level. He never
went to a public school or university. His father, Isaac D'Israeli,
was an author: respectable and comfortably off, but somewhat
detached. His grandfather, a Jewish merchant, had come to
England in 1748, only two generations before Benjamin's birth.
With his usual courage and self-confidence Disraeli never ob-
scured his Jewish origins, but made an asset of them: he believed
in race and regarded the Jewish race as the greatest of all. Without
any real justification[1] he decided that he was not only a Jew, but
an exceptionally aristocratic Jew, fully entitled to hold his own
with—or even to look down upon—the British nobility. Armed
with this conviction he could enter the saloons of Mayfair and
Belgravia without any sense of social inferiority.

There are occasional moods in Disraeli's novels when society
appears hollow or shallow. Tancred leaves its chatter for the Holy
Land. Egremont in *Sybil* (the most democratic of Disraeli's books)
experiences 'the People' in the persons of Sybil, her father and
Stephen Morley, and afterwards dwells in quite a Dickensian way
on the heartless vulgarity of the fashionable world and its failure
to feel and think. A passage in *Coningsby* contrasts English society

[1] Cf. Chapter 1 of Robert Blake's *Disraeli*.

unfavourably with French and praises the respect paid to intellect in Paris: 'In England when a new character appears in our circles, the first question always is, "Who is he?" In France it is "What is he?" In England, "How much a year?" In France, "What has he done?"'

But more often the note is one of interest or enjoyment. Except for some glimpses of working-class life in *Sybil*, and occasional visits to middle-class homes (like those of Mr. Putney Giles in *Lothair* and Mr. Job Thornberry in *Endymion*) the *milieu* of every book—and almost every scene—is aristocratic. Even the revolutionaries in *Lothair* are impeccably social. Somebody in *Lothair*, talking of the opera, notices how one never sees anybody there whom one saw before: '. . . it shows what a mass of wealth and taste and refinement there is in this wonderful metropolis of ours, quite irrespective of the circles in which we move, and which we once thought entirely engrossed them.'

This typically 'in-group' passage throws an interesting sidelight on the broadening of middle-class culture that had taken place since Disraeli's own youth. In *Endymion* he recalls the dull life of the middle classes in the London of 1830 and their restricted opportunities for entertainment. He also contrasts the society of that time with what it had become in his old age. In his youth manners were more stately and agreeable and conversation more cultivated. But the circle was more restricted and sympathies more contracted. More great houses were open, but very few little ones; there was less private entertainment:

'The great world then, compared with the huge society of the present period, was limited in its proportions, and composed of elements more refined though far less various. It consisted mainly of the great landed aristocracy, who had quite absorbed the nabobs of India, and had nearly appropriated the huge West Indian fortunes. Occasionally an eminent banker or merchant invested a large portion of his accumulations in land, and in the purchase of parliamentary influence, and was in due time admitted to the sanctuary. But those vast and successful invasions of society by new classes which have since occurred, though impending, had not yet commenced. The manufacturers, the railway kings, the colossal contractors, the discoverers of nuggets, had not yet found their place in society and the senate.'

As the century wore on it became less imperative to turn other forms of property into land; but landed wealth remained more acceptable socially than any other. In *Lothair* the Duke respects the American Colonel Campian as a Southern gentleman, having 'no property but land'. He tells his fellow-guests: 'You know he is a gentleman, he is not a Yankee.' St. Aldegonde, himself heir to the wealthiest British dukedom, was 'a republican of the reddest dye.' He was 'strongly in favour of the equal division of all property, except land. Liberty depended on land, and the greater the landowners, the greater the liberty of a country. He would hold forth on this topic even with energy, amazed at anyone differing from him; "as if a fellow could have too much land", he would urge with a voice and a glance which defied contradiction'.

Secure in his own knowledge of society Disraeli caricatured Thackeray, in *Endymion*, as the amusing, but socially envious, St. Barbe, who 'believed that literature and the arts, and intellect generally, had as little to hope for from one party as from the other.' He makes him exclaim: 'I hardly know which is the worst class in this country—the aristocracy, the middle class, or what they call the people. I hate them all.' Lord Montfort, fascinated by St. Barbe's *Topsy Turvy*, finds it 'very cynical, which authors, who know a little of the world, are apt to be, and everything is very exaggerated, which is another of their faults when they are only a trifle acquainted with manners. . . .' Later in *Endymion* Disraeli himself neatly ratifies this judgement: '. . . if the knowledge of society in its pages was not so distinguished as that of human nature generally, this was a deficiency obvious only to a comparatively limited circle of its readers.'

Society bulks large in Disraeli's novels, perhaps not least because he knew that it would help to make them sell. But the action is not entirely confined to great country houses or to the 'park or so, two or three squares, and a dozen streets where society lives; where it dines and dances, and blackballs, and bets, and spouts'. There are sketches of secluded, though still well-bred, country life in *Venetia* and in *Henrietta Temple*. There are excursions to the Near East in *Tancred* and *Lothair*. Conscious of the North/South problem both Coningsby and Endymion travel to exotic Manchester and are impressed by the importance, power and vitality of the new manufacturing England.

Social questions are tackled most seriously in *Coningsby* and *Sybil*. Together with *Tancred* they formed what Disraeli regarded as 'a real Trilogy; that is to say, they treat of the same subject, and endeavour to complete that treatment. The origin and character of our political parties, their influence on the condition of the people of this country, some picture of the moral and physical condition of that people, and some intimation of the means by which it might be elevated and improved, were themes which had long engaged my meditation'.[1] Tancred's object is to penetrate 'the great Asian mystery' of race and religion. Assured by his father that, what with the new railroads, 'even the condition of the poor, which I admit was lately far from satisfactory, is infinitely improved . . .', he is free to concentrate on moral elevation and to travel to the Holy Land in search of faith. *Sybil* deals with 'the condition of the people'; *Coningsby* with 'the origin and character of our political parties'. All three books attack the exclusive character of the Whig oligarchy and the heartless materialism of *laissez-faire* economics. They preach a revival of faith and sentiment, rising living standards for the people and the development of 'a generous aristocracy round a real throne'. Their central principle is that 'the tenure of property should be the fulfilment of duty'.

The three novels of the Trilogy were political propaganda. They did indeed express convictions held by Disraeli at the time; some of these convictions he continued to hold. But they were also the manifesto of the neo-feudal *Young England* movement, which wanted the aristocracy and clergy to lead and succour the people. *Young England* sighed for the antique and picturesque; it evoked the days of Laud and Charles I or, with pre-Raphaelite intensity, urged a revival of medieval faith and jollity. Typical of the movement was Lord Henry's indignation in *Coningsby* about an agricultural petition: 'Of course, I described it as the petition of the nobility, clergy, gentry, yeomanry and peasantry . . . and, could you believe it, they struck out *peasantry* as a word no longer used, and inserted *labourers*?' Typical also was the alms-giving ceremony on the estate of the young Roman Catholic proprietor, Eustace Lyle:

[1] From the General Preface to his collected novels, written in October, 1870.

'They came along the valley, a procession of Nature, whose groups an artist might have studied. The old man, who loved the pilgrimage too much to avail himself of the privilege of a substitute accorded to his gray hairs, came in person with his grandchild and his staff. There also came the widow with her child at the breast, and others clinging to her form; some sorrowful faces, and some pale; many a serious one, and now and then a frolic glance; many a dame in her red cloak, and many a maiden with her light basket; curly-headed urchins with demure looks, and sometimes a stalwart form baffled for a time of the labour he desired. But not a heart there that did not bless the bell that sounded from the tower of St. Genevieve!'

Even the style of this passage (studded with the words 'pilgrimage', 'staff', 'dame' and 'maiden') captures the revivalist and antiquarian mood of Early Victorian Gothic.

Disraeli was not perhaps over-popular with his fellow novelists and *Young England* was satirized both by Dickens and by Thackeray. Some of the ladies and gentlemen at Chesney Wold, in *Bleak House*, 'would make the vulgar very picturesque and faithful by putting back the hands upon the clock of time'. The red-faced, past-loving gentleman in *The Chimes* was originally to have been a *Young England* partisan.[1] In Thackeray's *Book of Snobs* the young De Mogyns, who has joined *Young England*, is 'the only man in the country who believes in the De Mogynses and sighs for the days when a De Mogyns led the van of battle. He has written a little volume of spoony puny poems. He wears a lock of the hair of Laud, the Confessor and Martyr, and fainted when he kissed the Pope's toe at Rome. He sleeps in white kid gloves and commits dangerous excesses upon green tea.' Even Kingsley, though evidently impressed and influenced by *Coningsby* and *Sybil*, and ready to represent *Young England* quite sympathetically in the person of Lord Vieuxbois, has reservations about the movement. In *Yeast* the hero 'could not help thinking of that amusingly inconsistent, however well-meant, scene in *Coningsby*, in which Mr. Lyle is represented as trying to restore "the independent order of peasantry', by making them the receivers of public alms at his own

[1] Cf. p. 80 above. See p. 530 of Edgar Johnson's *Charles Dickens*.

gate, as if they had been middle-age serfs or vagabonds, and not citizens of modern England.'

Disraeli himself was never wholly immersed in *Young England*. The central themes of the Trilogy are consistent with the ideas of the movement, but go beyond them. One of the themes is the importance of the established clergy as an instrument of national renovation. The Church, exemplified in the saintly and fascinating St. Lys, has a star role in *Sybil*; it is shown to have been the natural protector of the poor before the despoiling of its estates at the Reformation. Disraeli basically regarded religion as a department of politics; his hopes were soon shattered by Newman's secession to Rome, which he regarded as an inexplicable 'mistake' and 'misfortune' from which the Church of England never really recovered.

A still more central theme in *Sybil* is the need to improve working-class conditions. Disraeli had had an opportunity of studying correspondence between the chief actors of the Chartist movement. 'I had visited and observed with care all the localities introduced, and as an accurate and never exaggerated picture of a remarkable period in our domestic history, and of a popular organisation which in its extent and completeness has perhaps never been equalled, the pages of SYBIL may, I venture to believe, be consulted with confidence.' Factual accuracy was not always Disraeli's strongest point. But there is no reason to doubt his descriptions of distress in the manufacturing town of Mowbray and of squalor in the agricultural town of Marney. The misery of the hand-loom weaver in Mowbray, the injustice of the miners' 'tommy shop', the heartless theories of Lord Marney, the godless ignorance and brutality of Wogate: these are paralleled by similar exposures by Mrs. Gaskell, Dickens and Kingsley. One gets the impression that Disraeli had not often conversed with working men, or listened to them, for any length of time; but he does sometimes strike an authentic note—and, authentic or not, his descriptions avoid condescension. The scenes in which teenage Dandy Mick and his girl friends relax at the Temple of the Muses in Mowbray are sprightly, even if the girls only need a little more polish to talk like Countesses. Much of the book has a genuinely radical flavour. Sybil's father, Gerard, is made to say: 'There are great bodies of the working classes of this country nearer the condition of brutes than

88

they have been at any time since the Conquest.' Already interested
in Race, Disraeli draws a contrast between the 'Saxon industry' of
the peasantry and the 'Norman manners' inherited, or acquired, by
the upper class. Sybil begins by thinking of the people as Saxon
and the rich as Norman conquerors.

There is no hint of this distress when, years later, Lothair's
coming of age is celebrated at his country seat. Harmony seems to
reign between all classes. Not that much is seen of any class except
the highest. But 'farmers and townsmen and honest folk' are all
cheerfully present at Lothair's *levée*, where St. Aldegonde is especially pleased to meet a party of train stokers. Twenty years of calm
prosperity may not have brought the classes nearer together, but
at least the tensions between them have become less obtrusive.

Like all Disraeli's works the three novels of the Trilogy have a
strong aristocratic bias. The heroes are all aristocrats. Egremont,
in *Sybil*, marries the heroine; but, though apparently sprung from
the working class, she turns out to be an aristocrat herself. All
three books are redolent with a romantic love of blood and lineage.
Disraeli could feel a radical urge to reform and improve. He could
admire talented self-made men (like Mr. Vigo in *Endymion*) and he
had a genuine sympathy with the wrongs of the labouring classes.
But he was seldom a friend to the middle class as such or a spon-
taneous admirer of the virtues of method and routine. Dandy
Mick's friend Julia says in *Sybil*: 'If we can't have our own man, I
am all for the Nobs against the Middle Class'. The idea of an
alliance between Nobs and working men always had an appeal for
Disraeli.

But there is a curious ambivalence in Disraeli's attitude towards
the aristocracy in *Coningsby* and *Sybil*. In his later novels, *Lothair*
and *Endymion*, the aristocracy is taken for granted. So it is even in
Tancred, where the hero's father, the Duke of Bellamont, is an
amiable, innocent, rather retiring man, who at any rate on one side
can claim descent from 'a celebrated race of the times of the Plan-
taganets.' The unworldly Tancred feels that the aristocracy has
become degraded under the materialist influence of the age; but he
feels this still more strongly of the middle class, inevitably absorbed in making money. In an earlier novel, *Henrietta Temple*, the
young Marquis of Montfort is described as 'an excellent specimen
of a class inferior in talents, intelligence, and accomplishments, in

public spirit and in private virtues, to none in the world—the English nobility.'

In *Coningsby* and *Sybil*, however, a more critical note is struck. There is still the same feeling for blood: the same assumption that old blood has an automatic tendency to raise the tone of a man. The Duke of Beaumanoir in *Coningsby*, who 'had many of the virtues of his class: a few of their failings', comes from a genuinely old family. 'His good breeding . . . sprang from the only sure source of gentle manners, a kind heart. To have pained others would have pained himself. Perhaps, too, this noble sympathy may have been in some degree prompted by the ancient blood in his veins, an accident of lineage rather rare with the English nobility'. Mr. Trafford, the enlightened manufacturer in *Sybil*, is of old, Roman Catholic stock: 'With gentle blood in his veins, and old English feelings, he imbibed at an early period of his career a correct conception of the relations which should subsist between the employer and the employed'. Lord Valentine, proud that his family has 'mainly and materially assisted in making England what it is', appears as a real aristocrat. Sybil's father—a skilled working man, though himself of gentle blood—approves the young Lord's courtesy and feels an instinctive sympathy, when he calls on him as a delegate of the National Convention. Lord Valentine's family is old: although only ennobled for nearly three centuries, it bore 'a knightly name' before that.

But other aristocrats in these two books are less sympathetic and the origins of their families less truly noble. The aristocracy as a whole is criticized as a 'factitious aristocracy' or 'pseudo-aristocracy', shrinking from real leadership and all too often of recent lineage and bogus pedigree. Even its physical attributes are inadequate: 'There is no longer in fact an aristocracy in England, for the superiority of the animal man is an essential quality of aristocracy. But that it once existed, any collection of portraits from the 16th Century will show.' As to its public spirit, there is an acid reference to 'those toilsome patricians whose assiduity in affairs had convinced their unprivileged fellow-subjects that government was a science, and administration an art, which demanded the devotion of a peculiar class in the state for their fulfilment and pursuit.' Mr. Millbank, the manufacturer in *Coningsby*, who is against both an 'artificial equality' and a 'factitious aristocracy' and who brings up his son in the belief 'that he belonged to a class debarred from its just position in the social system', finds the existing upper class sadly wanting: not better informed than its inferiors, nor wiser, nor privately or publicly more virtuous, nor even of longer descent. 'I never heard of a peer' he says 'with ancient lineage. The real old families of this country are to be found among the peasantry; the gentry, too, may lay some claim to old blood.'

The plea, then, is for a 'real' aristocracy, 'a natural one'. But how was it to be composed? Disraeli is always better at posing riddles than at answering them. But, when he visited Manchester, Coningsby perceived that the new wealth 'was rapidly developing classes whose power was imperfectly recognised in the constitutional scheme, and whose duties in the social scheme seemed altogether omitted.' There is another clue in Disraeli's own comment towards the end of the book: 'Brains every day become more precious than blood. . . . Greatness no longer depends on rentals, the world is too rich; nor on pedigree, the world is too knowing.'

Disraeli's imagination responded easily to new ideas. They were not always fully compatible with each other and it was sometimes more convenient, politically, that their implications should not by pushed, or explored, too far. He was torn between Blood and Brains. Where he could, he combined them. He could be comfortable in the conviction that he combined them in himself.

The final message of *Sybil* foreshadows the 'property-owning democracy' of later Conservative thought. Sybil comes to ascribe 'the want of sympathy that unquestionably exists between Wealth and Work in England, to mutual ignorance between the classes'. Egremont tells her:

'The future principle of English politics will not be a levelling principle; not a principle adverse to privileges, but favourable to their extension. It will seek to ensure equality, not by levelling the Few, but by elevating the Many.'

'Levelling up' was also KINGSLEY's panacea. The gamekeeper Tregarva, in *Yeast*, says that he does not 'want to pull down any man to my level; I despise my level too much; I want to rise; I want those like me to rise with me. Let the rich be as rich as they

will.—I and those like me, covet not money, but manners.' Alton
Locke thinks that the working class could begin to look like
gentlemen given 'air, water, exercise, education, good society.'
He wants to see the grace of the fine lady 'extend to the labourer's
hovel and the needlewoman's garret.'

Kingsley was more genuinely democratic than Disraeli. Neo-
feudalism had less charm for him; his own inspiration was the
ideal of Christian brotherhood. He had more feeling for 'liberal
principles'; he was less susceptible to old blood and old manners;
he did not share Disraeli's preference for 'the use of ancient forms
and the restoration of the past'. But in other respects there was a
similarity between their social outlooks. Both emphasized the
social distress prevailing in the 1840s and the need to raise the
condition of the people. Kingsley was a dedicated sanitary reformer from his youth, while the elderly Disraeli took refuge in
sanitas sanitatum. Both believed (though Disraeli only for a time)
that the Church could do much to help. Lady Ellerton in *Alton
Locke* says that the clergy were formerly 'the only bulwark of the
poor against the mediaeval tyranny of Rank; you will find them the
only bulwark against the modern tyranny of Mammon'. Both
wanted the upper class to relieve and guide their fellows. 'The
working man has no want for real reverence . . .', we learn in
Alton Locke, 'it is the artisan's intense longing to find his real lords
and guides, which makes him despise and execrate his sham ones.'
Near the end of the book Alton Locke exclaims: 'Oh, my brothers,
my brothers! Little you know how many a noble soul, among those
ranks which you consider only as your foes, is yearning to love, to
help, to live and die for you, did they but know the way!' By the time
of *Two Years Ago* the American, Stangrave, finds it 'very hopeful,
to see your aristocracy joining in the general movement, and
bringing their taste and knowledge to bear on the lower classes.'

However radical in some of their sympathies, both Disraeli and
Kingsley were, in the last resort, Conservatives. For Lady Ellerton
Christ was 'the true Conservative', as well as 'the great Reformer'.
Kingsley became more conservative as he got older. The stable
fifties, after 'the hungry forties', must have tended to restore
complacency; perhaps, too, the upper classes had genuinely come
to feel more sense of social responsibility. Already, at the end of
Alton Locke, a letter from John Crosthwaite in Texas, dated

October 1848, refers to 'that fraternal union of all classes which I hear is surely, though slowly, spreading in my mother land'. Some years later, in the introductory part of *Two Years Ago*, Claude Mellot testifies:

'I knew this part of the country (Berkshire) well in 1846–7–8, and since then, I can bear witness, a spirit of self-reform has been awakened round here, in many a heart which I thought once utterly frivolous. I find, in every circle of every class, men and women asking to be taught their duty, that they may go and do it; I find everywhere schools, libraries, and mechanics' institutes springing up: and rich and poor meeting together more and more in the faith that God has made them all . . . since free trade and emigration, the labourers confess themselves better off than they have been for fifty years.'

In the 1859 Preface to the Fourth Edition of *Yeast* Kingsley welcomes 'the altered temper of the young gentlemen', particularly their changed tone towards the middle classes.

The influence of Disraeli's Trilogy is more marked in *Yeast* than in *Alton Locke*. Even in *Yeast* there are differences of approach: one obvious difference is that the hero, Lancelot Smith, is no aristocrat, but the son of a rich merchant. But the book has the romantic, picaresque, quality of *Coningsby* and *Sybil*. *Mutatis mutandis* the mysterious stranger, Barnakill, who at the end leads Lancelot to 'Jesus Christ—THE MAN', recalls the omniscient Sidonia who exercises such a spell over Coningsby.

The shadow of the Civil War hangs faintly over *Alton Locke* as it does over Disraeli's Trilogy. But, while in *Coningsby* Eustace Lyle is of 'an old Cavalier family' and St. Genevieve glories in having repelled the rebels, Alton's mother 'gloried in her dissent; for she was sprung from old Puritan blood'. The Cambridgeshire yeoman, who gives Alton a lift into the town, still had his forefather's sword and helmet at home: 'We was Parliament side— true Britons all we was, down into the fens and Oliver Cromwell, as dug Botsham lode, to the head of us.'

Yeast concentrates on rural distress in the South of England. Yet Kingsley's personal liking for the Southern countryman seems to have been lukewarm. He observes unenthusiastically of tenant farmers: 'I am bound to speak of the farmer, as I know him in the South of England. In the North he is a man of altogether higher education and breeding: but he is, even in the South, a much better man than it is the fashion to believe him.' Lancelot longs 'for some young sturdy Lancashire or Lothian blood, to put new life into the old frozen South Saxon veins! Even a drop of the warm enthusiastic Celtic would be better than none'. Tregarva, who becomes a friend of Lancelot and has the makings of a hero, is not a local man, but a Celt from Cornwall, with a considerable contempt for the 'stupid pigheaded' South countrymen. Kingsley presents the 'South Saxon' peasantry as a problem, rather than as people; one's hopes of really getting to know them are continually raised, but never fulfilled. When Lancelot finally goes with Tregarva to the village fair he hardly understands a word of the conversation, which sounds to him like 'the speech of savages', and is reduced to looking round the booth 'with a hopeless feeling'. The brief rural excursions in *Alton Locke* contrast the suspicious reserve of the agricultural labourer with the quick and passionate nature of the urban artisan.

Kingsley's peasantry is depressed and sluggish. His landowners may be inadequate; but they are not oppressive. He criticizes them for not doing enough to improve the basic conditions of rural life; but he recognizes that the better of them make a real effort of charity. Even Alton Locke acknowledges that visiting the sick and teaching in the schools are 'matters of course, not only in the families of clergymen, but those of most squires and noblemen, when they reside on their estates. . . .'

By contrast with *Yeast*, the scene of *Alton Locke* is mainly urban. Written in the first person by a cockney tailor/poet, son of a small retailer, it conveys a more concentrated and emphatic sense of social injustice than almost any Victorian novel. Alton, who gets involved in the Chartist movement, is acutely class-conscious; the kindly Dean, who interests himself in his poems, suggests that good and evil are pretty equally distributed among all ranks and exhorts him to give up 'the bitter tone against the higher classes which I am sorry to see in your MSS'. But the exhortation is only partly successful. The hero deeply resents the repressed condition of the lower class and recalls that it used to be the common people 'who heard Christ gladly'. Like George Eliot's Felix Holt he wants to stay in his own class, to regenerate and defend them, instead of becoming 'a sham gentleman' and a parasite, who will be complimented by the world on rising in life. He does not share, and has no sympathy with, his richer cousin's ambition to take the well-paved clerical road to social advancement.

Alton's cousin, like Kingsley himself, went to King's College, London, and then to Cambridge, before taking orders. But whereas his father had had to rise in the world and to make money as owner of 'a first-rate grocery establishment in the City', Kingsley did not need to go to Cambridge, or to take orders, to establish himself socially. His father was himself a clergyman and had originally been bred as a country gentleman. Kingsley's love of country sports, and of all the 'manly exercises' of the upper class, is evident in his work. He makes the delicate Alton Locke admire the 'grim, earnest, stubborn energy' of the Cambridge oarsmen and look wistfully at the happiness of the athletic gentleman/angler whose wood is the first that he has ever entered.

In spite of Alton Locke's fierce identification with his class it is the aristocratic Eleanor (Lady Ellerton) who in the end works his spiritual redemption and directs his thoughts from revolution to religion. But she and her husband are portrayed as exceptional aristocrats. Lord Scoutbush in *Two Years Ago*, although a nice young man, has nothing heroic about him. 'To do him justice', however, 'he was in one thing a true nobleman, for he was above all pride; as are most men of rank, who know what their own rank means. It is only the upstart, unaccustomed to his new eminence, who stands on his dignity and "asserts his power".' Grace Harvey, the poor and angelic schoolmistress in the same book, knew that all would be equal in heaven; meanwhile 'she found lords and ladies on earth, and seeing no open sin in the fact of their being richer and more powerful than she was, she supposed that God had put them where they were; and she accepted them simply as facts of His Kingdom. Of course they had their duties, as every one has: but what they were she did not know, or care to know.'

Kingsley neither worshipped, nor resented, the aristocracy; he wanted it to play its part—necessarily a leading part—in fostering Christian brotherhood. Though he admired gentleman-like and ladylike qualities, he longed to see them more widely diffused. Like Dickens he saw no reason why marriages between different classes should not turn out well. The doctor's son, Frank Thurnall, marries Grace Harvey; the squireen Trebooze, who 'would have crushed and ill-used a delicate and high-minded wife', has the sense to marry his housemaid. 'More than once has one seen the same seeming folly turn out in practice as wise a step as could well have been taken.' The ideal of Christian brotherhood may have encouraged some illusions about existing, or impending, class relations; but it saved Kingsley from the sense of caste that oppressed so many of his contemporaries.

*   *   *

Dickens and Disraeli had a flamboyant love of emphasis. Surtees, usually, and Dickens, sometimes, wrote for comic effect. Dickens, Disraeli and Kingsley were political propagandists: the first as a radical, the second as a Tory paternalist and the third as a 'muscular' and fraternal Christian. Hence much of what they wrote about social relations was exaggerated. But, even when exaggerated, it was often, in essence, true. Between them, the four novelists covered a wider ground than the women novelists and filled it with the vigour of the real world.

Surtees apart, these novels contain more explicit, and more bitter, criticism of the social system than those of the women novelists. But their criticism was never aimed at the total destruction of the system; nor did they question that to be a gentleman or a lady was, in one sense or another, a desirable thing.

In the work of the more realistic Thackeray and Trollope the importance of being 'gentle' becomes an inspiration, or obsession, central to the novelist's whole view of how people should behave.

5. *Edification*

It comes as a surprise to find that Thackeray and Trollope could have been boys at school together. Thackeray died younger and had something of the eighteenth century's spirit and style, while Trollope began writing rather late and in an eminently mid-Victorian manner. So they appear to belong to different generations, when in fact there were only four years between them. When one thinks of them as contemporaries, they make an obvious pair. They were both men of the world who tried to give a realistic picture of their own quarter of society. Trollope did not share Thackeray's fondness for 'Bohemia', while he had a better working knowledge of professional, rural and official life. But otherwise the two novelists worked the same social vein and, though both were professed liberals, had similar views as to how people should behave. The vigorous and prolific Trollope seldom aimed at Thackeray's irony, subtlety and style: he admired Thackeray's style, but at its plainest, finding it sometimes 'disfigured by a slight touch of affectation'. But both were capable of the same kind of sentiment. Both really lived with their characters (as Trollope observed of Thackeray) in their best work. Both loved generous youth and tender womanhood; and both admired exceedingly the idea of the English gentleman. Even in his feeling for the eighteenth century Thackeray was not so far removed from Trollope who, for all his mid-Victorianism, was most at home in that part of England which had remained closest to the eighteenth century in its behaviour and outlook.

The two men approached their work from the same stand-point, however different their methods. Both were natural story tellers, who were driven to write novels in order to make money. At the same time each felt a moral duty towards his public. Trollope regarded it as 'a matter of deep conscience' to the novelist 'how he shall handle those characters by whose words and doings he hopes to interest his readers. . . . How shall he teach lessons of virtue and at the same time make himself a delight to his readers?' 'Gentle readers', he confessed in *Ralph the Heir*, 'the physic is always beneath the sugar, hidden or unhidden. In writing novels we novelists preach to you from our pulpits, and are keenly anxious that our sermons shall not be inefficacious.' Thackeray parhaps tackled the problem less bluntly: but he wrote to a clergyman in 1850:

'I want . . . to say in my way, that love and truth are the greatest of Heaven's commandments and blessings to us; that the best of us, the many especially who pride themselves on their virtue most, are wretchedly weak, vain and selfish; and at least to preach such a charity, as a common sense of our shame and unworthiness might inspire to us poor people. I hope men of my profession do no harm who talk this doctrine out of doors to people in drawing-rooms and in the world.'

Trollope himself, in his *Autobiography*, gave Thackeray full marks for good principle:

'Among all his stories there is not one which does not leave on the mind a feeling of distress that women should ever be immodest or men dishonest—and of joy that women should be so devoted and men so honest. How we hate the idle selfishness of Pendennis, the worldliness of Beatrix, the craft of Becky Sharpe!—how we love the honesty of Colonel Newcome, the nobility of Esmond and the devoted affection of Mrs. Pendennis! The hatred of evil and love of good can hardly have come upon so many readers without doing much good.'

Thackeray would have valued this tribute, even though his feelings about his own characters can hardly have been so black and white. (No doubt he really did love Colonel Newcome and Mrs. Pendennis—though not all modern readers would be eager for their company—but he was clearly fond of Pendennis and cannot quite have hated Beatrix or Becky.) His notion of virtue may have been more supple than Trollope's; but he was certainly one with him in wanting to do his readers good. Thus, though both writers give a more rounded and balanced picture of life than the reformers and humorists discussed in the last chapter, they are by no means above a little propaganda and caricature themselves. A common desire to edify gives a pattern to their work and shapes the categories into which they place their characters and their characters' moods. Since both value what is gentlemanly as well as what is good—or perhaps find that, to be really graceful, goodness must be gentlemanly—this edification has a social, as well as a moral, tendency.

* * *

Many tributes have been paid to THACKERAY's realism. Leslie Stephen, his son-in-law, regarded him as 'a thorough realist' who for that reason 'refrained from descriptions of the classes of society with which he was not actually familiar': 'How far his portrait is correct is another question; but fidelity, not the production of a powerful effect, is the ultimate end, and a desire to see things as they are the governing and regulating principle of his work.' Thackeray's characters are recognisable types; they eschew violent eccentricity; they have familiar virtues and frailties; their experiences are such as most people of their class could share; they react and talk exactly as they ought; they move in the real world of London or elsewhere. They are, in short, real people and the more we think about them, the more we are likely to find them so. Yet the immediate impact which they make on the imagination is somehow less solid and less vivid than it is in retrospect.

Perhaps the basic reason for this curious illusion of thinness in Thackeray's delineation is the pervasiveness of his own personality in the writing (and, in the books which he illustrated himself, in the drawing). Throughout all the changes of scene and character the reader moves in the single, fluid, element of Thackeray's sensibility and discrimination; hence the *dramatis personae*, though not merely carefully observed but deeply imagined, seem diluted with at least one part of Thackeray to two parts of themselves. We are seldom allowed a real glimpse into the inner workings of their minds or shown them coming to a decision, even from the outside. On the other hand we get a great deal of *ex cathedra* commentary on their actions. It is only in the occasional scenes of dramatic action that they are really allowed to take charge. Otherwise, although they behave as their natures dictate, the author remains visibly in ultimate control, and we see everything through his eyes. He cannot make his creatures act out of character—they have too much life and truth for that—but he can make them pose whenever he wishes and keep them standing while he draws his moral.

It is not only Thackeray's rather leisurely way of shooting the scenes that softens the impact of his characters, but his constant habit of placing them in categories. His observation of them is always critical, even when it is kind. He is far too subtle and sympathetic to present his characters unmixed: the most saintly have human weaknesses and the most villainous have their tender moments. But his moral discrimination is continually in play. 'Here you see X, who is normally good, behaving badly because of the stupid or wicked prejudices of society' he seems to say, or 'Note how Y, though the truest-hearted creature alive, has the selfishness inseparable from her own pure passion', or 'The wicked Z, as you see, is not so far corrupt that he cannot love his child more dearly than some virtuous people might', or 'Here is dry, pompous, selfish, old W, who can nevertheless recognise and admire honourable conduct in others.'

This continual process of moral reflection and classification has of course a value of its own. It impresses on the reader Thackeray's own view of what standards should guide human behaviour: his dislike of hypocrisy, pomposity and materialism; his love of youth, tender old age, natural affection, high spirits, grace of feeling, etc. These standards may sometimes seem facile or sentimental; but they are honest and humane and, quite genuinely, edifying. There is no reason why a novelist should not seek to spread his moral gospel in this way, if that is what he chiefly wants to do. But he will have to make his creatures his servants, instead of allowing them to master him, and this must result in some loss of force and movement. The commentary, too, is liable to colour the action so as to give an impression of soft idealism on the one hand, or harsh caricature on the other, however true to life the action itself may be. This is exactly what happens in Thackeray's work, except when his imagination is at its most powerful, and takes full charge.

I dwell on this because Thackeray is as much a social classifier as a moral one. All his characters are put carefully into the social categories for which they are fitted by their birth, fortune, education, profession and tastes. We are continually being reminded, for instance, that the father of Ridley R.A. was a butler; that Miss

Honeyman, who keeps a boarding house, was a clergyman's daughter and considers herself a gentlewoman; that George Warrington, for all his radicalism, comes of an old family. This emphasis on class is of course not only compatible with, but essential to, a realistic picture of the society of the time. But it is so pronounced in Thackeray's work that it tends to have a rather deadening or flattening effect on his characters. This is particularly the case when he deals with his social superiors or inferiors. Some of his aristocrats (Lord Steyne, Lady Kew, Lord Ringwood) are strong characters; their good and bad points are fairly presented; they are not pasteboard figures. But we are never allowed to forget that they are aristocrats or to see them in social undress. The portraits may be good; but the frames are obtrusive. At the other end of the scale it is difficult to take Thackeray's lower middle class or lower class characters quite seriously, because they are always so audibly dropping or inserting aitches. The 'Little Sister' in *Philip* is touchingly drawn and almost an exception; but she does not forget her place. There is a sympathetic, even an admiring, portrait of the servant Dick Bedford in *Lovel the Widower*; but of him too the narrator has to say: 'Bedford had constantly to do battle with the aspirates. He conquered them, but you could see there was a struggle.' In the same kind of way the wealthy West Indian, Woolcomb, can never appear in *Philip* without some facetious, and not very liberal, reference to his dark complexion.

There is of course less social discrimination when Thackeray enters the carefree and relatively classless land of Bohemia (a 'pleasant land, not fenced with drab stucco, like Tyburnia or Belgravia') or when—as is most often the case—he has to do with his social equals. He was himself firmly rooted in the respectable upper middle class which, without pretending to nobility, was a good deal nearer to the upper class in manners and education than to the commercial bourgeoisie. His father and grandfather were both servants of the East India Company; his great-grandfather was a surgeon; his great-great-grandfather, descended from a family of West Riding yeomen, had been headmaster of Harrow. Physicians, clergymen and officers abounded in what was, in the eighteenth century, a prolific family. He himself inherited a fortune, which he lost while still a young man. He was educated at Charterhouse and Trinity, Cambridge; subsequently he travelled on the Continent, entered the Middle Temple, settled for a time in Paris, worked at art and finally took to writing to support his family.

Thackeray's attitude towards snobbery was complex. There was something Proustian about his awareness of class; there must have been a time in his youth when, like Proust, he was fired by a romantic ambition to scale the heights of society. 'What is the secret of great social success?' (he asks in *Philip*). 'It is not to be gained by beauty, or wealth, or birth, or wit, or valour, or eminence of any kind. It is a gift of Fortune, bestowed, like that goddess's favours, capriciously.' In his ironic way he relished the magic of noble names and titles, and exploited it conscientiously in his novels of the eighteenth century. For all his dislike of the *Peerage* he found the book 'a sort of gold-laced and liveried lackey to History, and in so far serviceable.' He did not avoid the good society to which his reputation as a writer introduced him. Like Becky Sharp, he could admire the grand manner. When Becky saw Lord Steyne for the last time in Rome, he was 'smiling sumptuously, easy, lofty and stately' and looking and speaking 'like a great prince, as he was'. Lady Ann Newcome says of her brother-in-law, the Colonel:

'Your uncle is adorable. I have never seen a more perfect *Grand Seigneur*. He puts me in mind of my grandfather, though grandpapa's grand manner was more artificial, and his voice spoiled by snuff. . . .'

Leslie Stephen, referring to the Snob Papers in the *Dictionary of National Biography*, says that Thackeray 'was occasionally accused of sharing the weakness which he satirised, and would playfully admit that the charge was not altogether groundless.' As author of these papers he called himself 'Mr. Snob' and playfully admitted, or pretended, that he would 'be ready to jump out of my skin if two Dukes would walk down Pall Mall with me.'

But, if Thackeray felt the magnetism of birth and social distinction, he was the more alive to the humbug which surrounded them. He allows a genuine lineage to one or two of his aristocrats, such as the good, stupid, Lady Grizel Macbeth in *Vanity Fair* who 'deplored the fatal levelling tendencies of the age': 'It is not her Ladyship's fault that she fancies herself better than you and me.

The skirts of her ancestors' garments have been kissed for centuries. . . .' In most cases, however, he seems to take a delight in showing up pedigrees as spurious and in revealing his nobility as *parvenu*. The formidable old Lady Kew goes so far as to say:

'Except the Gaunts, the Howards, and one or two more, there is scarcely any good blood in England. You are lucky in sharing some of mine. My poor Lord Kew's grandfather was an apothecary at Hampton Court, and founded the family by giving a dose of rhubarb to Queen Caroline. As a rule, nobody is of a good family.'

Awareness of his snobbery gave an edge to Thackeray's disgust with the power exercised by Birth and Wealth over English society at the time. His politics were liberal (in later life he was narrowly defeated as a parliamentary candidate for Oxford) and he described himself to his mother, in 1840, as a republican and against aristocratic government. He preferred the 'manly equality' in France to the relations 'between rich and poor in our own country, with all our superior wealth, instruction and political freedom'. In the early *Shabby Genteel Story* he attacks the 'accursed system' which is called in England 'the education of a gentleman' and which inculcates selfishness, snobbery and a contempt for 'natural tenderness'. Elsewhere in the same book he exclaims: 'O free and happy Britons, what a miserable, truckling, cringing race ye are!'

The *Book of Snobs*, which first really made Thackeray's reputation, contains his sharpest criticism of the social system. The touch was light, since the papers were written for *Punch*; but the intention was serious. Writing in 1859 Kingsley welcomed the altered tone of young gentlemen towards the middle classes 'and that word "snob" (thanks very much to Mr. Thackeray) used by them in its true sense, without regard of rank. . . .' Eighteenth-century slang for a shoemaker and Cambridge slang for a townsman, the word had come to be used about the lower classes generally. Thence it could be applied to someone of any class who was not a gentleman. Jack Belsize describes Barnes Newcome as 'A little snob. . . . I never heard him say a good word of any mortal soul, or do a kind action'. The modern definition of the word in the *Oxford English Dictionary* as one who 'meanly or vulgarly admires and seeks to imitate, or associate with, those of superior rank or wealth' seems to derive from Thackeray's own definition: 'He who meanly admires mean things is a Snob'. 'First the World was made', he says in his Prefatory Remarks, 'then, as a matter of course, Snobs; they existed for years and years, and were no more known than America. But presently,—*ingens patebat tellus*,—the people became darkly aware that there was such a race. Not above five-and-twenty years since, a name, an expressive monosyllable, arose to designate that race. . . . It is a great mistake to judge of Snobs lightly, and think they exist among the lower classes merely.'

The *Book of Snobs* is an attack on Toadyism, Mammon-worship, 'Lord-olatry', the Court Circular and keeping up with the Joneses. It finds British society deeply impregnated with snobbery. 'It is impossible for *any* Briton, perhaps, not to be a snob in some degree. If people can be convinced of this fact, an immense point is gained, surely. If I have pointed out the disease, let us hope that other scientific characters may discover the remedy.'

Mr. Snob does not blame the peerage as such; but he points out that it is difficult 'for the Snob's idol not to be a Snob' and that a nobleman 'may be an ass, and yet respected; or a ruffian and yet be exceedingly popular. . . .' '. . . it is not out of disrespect for the individuals, that I wish these titles had never been invented; but, consider, if there were no tree, there would be no shadow. . . .' However, finding the greatest profusion of Snobs among the *respectable* classes, he proceeds to get his teeth into City Snobs, Military Snobs, Clerical Snobs, University Snobs, Continental (travelling) Snobs, Dinner-giving Snobs, Country Snobs and Club Snobs. Although he cannot bring himself to cast too much ridicule on the clergy, or to disparage the gallantry of the Army, he criticizes aristocratic jobbery and patronage, the system of commission purchase and the division of undergraduates into different social ranks. But it is a change of heart as much as a reform of institutions that Mr. Snob urges on his brother Snobs:

'. . . it seems to me that all English society is cursed by this mammoniacal superstition; and that we are sneaking and boring and cringing on the one hand, or bullying and scorning on the other, from the lowest to the highest. . . . I can bear it no longer—this diabolical invention of gentility which kills natural kindliness and honest friendship. Proper pride, indeed! Rank and precedence, forsooth! The table of ranks and degrees is a lie, and should be flung into the fire. Organise ranks and precedence! that was well for the masters of ceremonies of former ages. Come forward, some great Marshal, and organise Equality in society, and your rod shall swallow up all the juggling old court goldsticks.'

Mr. Snob melts entirely into Thackeray in the two final paragraphs:

'I am sick of *Court Circulars*. I loathe *haut-ton* intelligence. I believe such words as Fashionable, Exclusive, Aristocratic, and the like, to be wicked, un-christian epithets, that ought to be banished from honest vocabularies. A Court system that sends men of genius to the second table, I hold to be a Snobbish system. A society that sets up to be polite, and ignores Arts and Letters, I hold to be a Snobbish Society. You, who despise your neighbour, are a Snob; you, who forget your own friends, meanly to follow after those of a higher degree, are a Snob; you, who are ashamed of your poverty, and blush for your calling, are a Snob; as are you who boast of your pedigree, or are proud of your wealth.'

'To laugh at such is *Mr. Punch*'s business. May he laugh honestly, hit no foul blow, and tell the truth when at his very broadest grin—never forgetting that if Fun is good, Truth is still better, and Love best of all.'

Thackeray remained a snob-baiter throughout his career as a novelist. But in time he became a little more forgiving of the Snob's failings and less acutely critical of the social system which bred Snobs in such abundance. *Vanity Fair* has some of the asperity of the Snob Papers; it refers, for instance, to 'that happy frigidity and insolence of demeanour which occasionally characterises the great at home' and describes the efforts to get tickets for the Waterloo Ball as being 'such as only English ladies will employ, in order to gain admission to the society of the great of their own nation.' But the action of *Vanity Fair* takes place about a generation previously and, if the book holds up a cracked (though unclouded) glass to human behaviour, it is in a mood of disillusion, rather than of reform. As usual in Thackeray's work good and bad are to be found at every social level; corruption is not confined to any particular rank or ranks; where individuals go wrong they do so because of their own natures, or because of the general tone of society, not because they are bound to do so as representatives of their class.

Pendennis is at once more mellow than the earlier *Vanity Fair* and more tart than the later *Newcomes*. Major Pendennis's social pretensions come in for their full share of ridicule and his merits, though not skimped, are never fully admitted. Nothing is more typical of Thackeray than the way in which the Major manages to survive, battered and unbowed, his creator's continual efforts to put him in his place. However, the masculine honours of the book go to George Warrington, who is bored by his own class:

'"In society everybody is the same, wears the same dress, eats and drinks and says the same things; one young dandy at the club talks and looks like another, one Miss at a ball exactly resembles another. . . . I like to talk with the strongest man in England, or the man who can drink the most beer in England, or with that tremendous republican of a hatter, who thinks Thistlewood was the greatest character in history. I like gin-and-water better than claret. I like a sanded floor in Carnaby Market better than a chalked one in Mayfair. I prefer Snobs.¹ I own it." Indeed this gentleman was a social republican; and it never entered his head while conversing with Jack and Tom that he was in any respect their better; although, perhaps the deference which they paid him might secretly please him.'

The qualification in the last sentence is extremely characteristic of the way in which Thackeray blends vinegar with his oil.

There is some heavy 'republican' irony in the following passage:

'This fact shows our British independence and honest feeling—our higher orders are not such mere haughty aristocrats as the ignorant represent them: on the contrary, if a man have money they will hold out their hands to him, eat his dinners, dance at his balls, marry his daughters, or give their own lovely girls to his sons, as affably as your commonest roturier would do.'

But the glimpses of the great world in *Pendennis* and the later

¹ Here meaning the unabashed vulgar, in the pre-Thackerayan sense.

novels seem to suggest more familiarity and more tolerance than when the author of *Vanity Fair* wrote: 'As I cannot describe the mysteries of Freemasonry, although I have a shrewd idea that it is a humbug, so an uninitiated man cannot take upon himself to portray the great world accurately, and had best keep his opinions to himself whatever they are.'

In a debate with Warrington Pendennis deprecates revolutionary ardour and says that he waits 'for time and truth to develop, or fortify, or (if you like) destroy' existing institutions. He observes of the aristocratic order:

'There it is, extant among us, a part of our habits, the creed of many of us, the growth of centuries, the symbol of a most complicated tradition—there stand my lord the bishop and my lord the hereditary legislator—what the French call *transactions* both of them. . . . I acquiesce that they exist, and no more . . . if they are to die, I would rather they had a decent and a natural than an abrupt and violent death.'

Warrington regards Pendennis as worldly and nobody quite has the last word in this debate; but Thackeray seems increasingly to have sided with Pendennis in tolerating tradition, while awaiting reform.

Almost the chief theme of *The Newcomes* (and a theme of *Philip* as well) was foreshadowed in the *Book of Snobs*: the wrongness of marrying for money or position and of allowing lack of fortune to frustrate love matches. The heroine, Ethel, is saved by her grandmother's death and her own better nature from making a 'brilliant' marriage with the Marquess of Farintosh. She had already exclaimed to her grandmother (Lady Kew): 'There never were, since the world began, people so unblushingly sordid! We own it, and are proud of it. We barter rank against money, and money against rank, day after day.' This theme is developed to the full in *The Newcomes* and not only in regard to Ethel. But there is no real attack on the class system in general, or on the upper class in particular. Lady Ann Newcome is more sympathetic than her sister-in-law, Mrs. Hobson, who holds intellectual *soirées* in Bryanston Square and, as 'a merchant's wife and an attorney's daughter' refuses to 'bow down to kiss the hand of a haughty aristocracy'. The young Lord Kew (like Philip Debarry in *Felix Holt*) 'showed no difference in his conversation with men of any degree, except, perhaps, that to his inferiors in station he was a little more polite than to his equals'. He and his kind get an ungrudging tribute: 'A young nobleman, full of life and spirits, generous of his money, jovial in his humour, ready with his sword, frank, handsome, prodigal, courageous, always finds favour.'

By the time of *Philip*, although Thackeray's values are basically unchanged, his acceptance of the social system has perhaps progressed still further. The 'worldly' but kind-hearted Pendennis, caricatured by the slanderous Mr. Trail as 'a parasite of the nobility', is his mouthpiece in this book. Admitting that he at one time took a little pleasure in being thought 'a dangerous man', Pendennis deploys all his creator's ambiguous irony in deprecating his present moderation:

'Now I am ready to say that Nero was a monarch with many elegant accomplishments, and considerable natural amiability of disposition. I praise and admire success wherever I meet it. I make allowance for faults and shortcomings, especially in my superiors; and feel that, did we know all, we should judge them very differently. People don't believe me, perhaps, quite as much as formerly. But I don't offend: I trust I don't offend.'

The harmless snobbery of the artist Ridley is handled gently: 'I believe his pedigree gave him secret anguishes. He would rather have been gentleman than genius ever so great; but let you and me, who have no weaknesses of our own, try and look charitably on this confessed foible of my friend.' Philip himself, though a radical in his opinions and 'one of the half-dozen men I have seen in my life upon whom rank made no impression', is 'not a little proud of some of his ancestors.' (Equally George Warrington, re-appearing in *The Newcomes*, was inclined to brag about his pedigree 'under certain influences', notably claret.) Sir John Ringwood, regarding himself as 'a staunch liberal' and boasting of 'going with the age', says that '. . . family . . . and ancestors, and what we have not done ourselves, these things we can hardly call ours.' But he is satirized for not applying his egalitarian views to his own treatment of his servants.

Even in the ardour of his youth Thackeray was scarcely a revolutionary. He disliked having to kowtow to the peerage—although it fascinated him—and he disliked seeing others do so. At least at one time he would have done away with the hereditary principle in the legislature, opened the services to talent and torn up the table of precedence. He would have had people treat each other with civility, but no more, and live honestly and unaffectedly within their means. But there is nothing to show that he believed in a radical redistribution of wealth or wished to dismantle the barriers of politeness and education. He seems to have been less actively interested in giving the lower classes wider opportunities, than in loosening the framework of the middle and upper ranks of society and promoting greater freedom of address between all classes. Perhaps he had in mind a model of French society as it was under the July monarchy, when the hold of the aristocracy had been twice shaken and outward forms had been democratized, but there was no real challenge to the higher *bourgeoisie* from less educated classes. One of his complaints in the *Book of Snobs* was about the low place officially allotted to Arts and Letters in English society. Here, certainly, he had the French example in mind. He wanted to rid the social system of the relics of feudalism, on the one hand, and excessive materialism, on the other; but there is little to suggest that his reforms would have gone much further than that. Later in his life, though he was still an enemy of snobbish materialism, he was perhaps in no hurry even to go that far.

In one respect, indeed, Thackeray was always something of a traditionalist. Whatever his views about the aristocracy he cherished closely the ideal of the 'gentleman'. Those of his characters who approach most nearly to this ideal are not necessarily of distinguished family. Dobbin was the son of a successful grocer, while Colonel Newcome was quite aware that his family's pedigree had been faked. On the other hand birth is no hindrance and, where it is present, seems to confer an added grace. Lord Kew is an aristocrat; so was Philip Brandon's mother; George Warrington comes of an old family. The eccentric Bayham in *The Newcomes* retains some of the characteristics of a gentleman, his family having been 'gentlefolks when many a fine lord's father of the present day was sweeping a counting-house.' Colonel Newcome, talking to his son of the spurious Newcome lineage, says:

'I think every man would like to come of an ancient and honourable race. . . . As you like your father to be an honourable man, why not your grandfather, and his ancestors before him? But if we can't inherit a good name, at least we can do our best to leave one. . . .'

Thackeray's gentlemen were not obliged to be well-born; but they had to have the speech, manners and education of their class. They were required to pass a stiffer moral, than social, examination; but some social qualifications were indispensable. A capacity to speak in blank verse was needed to sustain the dignity of the part, and this could hardly be cultivated in low company. Colonel Newcome, though 'the kindest and simplest soul alive', yet 'disliked all familiarity, and expected from common people the sort of deference which he had received from his men in the regiment.' He thought that 'a young man whose father may have had to wait behind me at dinner, should not be brought into my company.' This was natural enough in an Indian Army officer. But even the 'social republican' Warrington says to Pendennis, referring to their laundress and housemaid: '. . . a high-souled man doesn't make friends of these. A gentleman doesn't choose these for his companions or bitterly rues it afterwards if he do.' Philip, another radical who has no respect for rank, does not care to be on intimate terms with his employer, the newspaperman Mugford, who 'never professed the least gentility', used his knife as a fork and was indifferent to aspirates. Philip admits Mrs. Mugford to be a good woman, but asks how his wife can 'frankly be the friend of a woman who calls a drawing-room a droaring-room? With our dear little friend in Thornhaugh Street,[1] it is different. She makes no pretence even at equality. Here is a patron and patroness, don't you see?' Although he is talking to the saintly Laura Pendennis, she does not reprove him.

How does Philip escape the imputation of snobbery? If we are not 'meanly to admire mean things', should we meanly despise things that are only trivially mean? Or are we right to insist on our own standards, however exclusive, so long as we do not ape those of our superiors? The moral seems lacking and there is nothing to show whether Thackeray himself felt the inconsistency. Perhaps he

[1] The 'Little Sister'. Cf. p. 101 above.

did feel it, but knew that that was how Philip would behave and did not care to lecture him for such natural weakness. Or perhaps he regarded the ordinary standards of gentlemanly speech and conduct as being too basic to incur the reproach of 'this diabolical invention of gentility which kills natural kindliness and honest friendship'.

We are left with a vivid picture of Philip speaking and Laura listening and Thackeray smiling, kindly and ambiguously, from the wings. If any moral can be drawn from this completely realistic little scene, it is that there were limits to 'social republicanism' in Thackeray's world and that even his gentlemen could be—and perhaps could not avoid being—snobs.

* * *

TROLLOPE's characters seem to have more flesh and blood than Thackeray's because he shows us more of the workings of their minds and not quite so much of his own. His world is, at first sight, more real. Yet there is a deeper sense in which it is less realistic. Although Thackeray seeks to edify his readers by discriminating between true and false values, he does not pretend that virtue is necessarily loved and rewarded, or that vice and selfishness cannot, in a worldly way, prosper. He is guided by true imagination, not by morality, in working out the fates of his characters. Trollope, on the other hand, harnesses his extremely realistic technique quite deliberately to moral ends. He says in his *Autobiography*:

'I have always desired to "hew out some lump of the earth", and to make men and women walk upon it just as they do walk here among us,—with not more of excellence, nor with exaggerated baseness. . . . If I could do this, then I thought I might succeed in impregnating the mind of the novel-reader with a feeling that honesty is the best policy; that truth prevails while falsehood fails; that a girl will be loved, as she is pure, and sweet and unselfish; that a man will be honoured as he is true, and honest and brave of heart; that things meanly done are ugly and odious, and things nobly done beautiful and gracious.'

Life can be difficult for the good in Trollope's novels, but not permanently intolerable. The bad are sure to come to grief sooner or later—though they may not be unmitigatedly bad and their grief may not be total. Poor Crosbie, in *The Small House at Allington*, behaves really badly when he proposes to Lady Alexandrina de Courcy so soon after being accepted by Lily Dale. But he pays for his sin in the most remorseless way. Not only is his brief married life unbelievably dreary, but a permanent blight descends on his financial and social prospects. Nothing in Trollope's treatment of this story is so exaggerated as to be out of key; but everything in it has clearly been contrived to produce a certain effect. The same could be said of Alaric Tudor's financial degradation in *The Three Clerks*. If the machinery does not creak more loudly it is because Trollope is usually careful to maintain his characters on a familiar level of experience. Even when it comes to drawing morals he keeps his sense of proportion and his awareness of what is, or can be, done.

The ugliness of 'things meanly done' and the beauty of 'things nobly done': Trollope's use of these words suggests an aesthetic approach to morality, which explains a good deal in his social outlook. Like Thackeray he treasured the ideal of the English gentleman. None of the major Victorian novelists dwells more often, or more lovingly, on the characteristics that make men gentlemen and women ladies. When he draws on lower middle class life (for instance the commercial travellers in *Orley Farm*) his descriptions are human and observant; but there is no real engaging of sympathy. His rather infrequent excursions into the lower strata of society—seldom the lowest—are largely for comic effect or in order to point a contrast. Now and then he takes us into seedy public houses, or shabby genteel boarding houses; but they remind him unpleasantly of the days before his success and he does not stay long there. Of course his low life characters can be good and bad, can feel and suffer and rejoice, like their superiors; sometimes they deserve as much, or more respect; but there is a kind of tacit understanding between the novelist and his readers that they are not to be taken quite so seriously. Heroes and heroines, even when not excessively heroic, come from the world of ladies and gentlemen. To avoid meanness and ugliness requires not only virtue, but also education and manners, if not blood.

What Trollope meant by describing people or conduct as 'gentlemanly' or 'ladylike' will be looked at more closely in the next chapter. But the following passage from his *Autobiography* shows his general approach. Referring to Thackeray's portrait of Colonel Newcome he exclaims:

'How great a thing it is to be a gentleman at all parts! How we admire the man of whom we feel sure that so much may be said with truth! It is not because Colonel Newcome is a perfect gentleman that we think Thackeray's work to have been so excellent, but because he has had the power to describe him as such, and to force us to love him, a weak and silly old man, on account of this grace of character.'

The 'grace of character' that Trollope admires depends on social as well as moral refinement. Theodore Burton in *The Claverings* is a good man; but he puts off Harry Clavering by dusting his shoes with his handkerchief.

Trollope's own social preference is confessed in his *Autobiography*:

'I do not scruple to say that I prefer the society of distinguished people, and that even the distinction of wealth confers many advantages. . . . The graces come easier to the wife of him who has had great-grandfathers . . . the society of the well-born and of the wealthy will as a rule be worth seeking.'

Mr. Vavasor advises his daughter in *Can You Forgive Her?*:

'. . . you may be sure of this, that men and women ought to grow, like plants, upwards. Everybody should endeavour to stand as well as he can in the world and if I had a choice of acquaintance between a sugar-baker and a peer, I should prefer the peer,— unless, indeed, the sugar-baker had something very strong on his side to offer. I don't call that tuft-hunting and it does not necessitate toadying. It's simply growing up, towards the light, as the trees do.'

If there is irony in this passage it is a defensive irony that enables Trollope to put forward his own views in a slightly deprecatory way. That they are, in essence, his own views is confirmed by a reading of his novels as a whole. It is because of his manly aversion from 'tuft-hunting' and 'toadying', because of his lack of inverted snobbery, because of something frank and blunt in his social outlook, that Trollope escapes the charge of snobbery. No doubt he escapes it better than Thackeray, though he was far less inclined to criticize the social system. The difference between the two men is well brought out by Trollope himself, in a passage in *He Knew He Was Right*, when he describes the American Mrs. Spalding's delight at her niece having married a lord:

'. . . in accordance with the teaching which we got,—alas, now many years ago,—from a great master on the subject, we must conclude that poor, dear, Mrs. Spalding was a snob. Nevertheless, with all deference to the memory of that great master, we think that Mrs. Spalding's allusions to the success in life achieved by her niece were natural and altogether pardonable; and that reticence on the subject . . . would have betrayed on the whole a condition of mind lower than that she exhibited. While rank, wealth and money are held to be good things by all around us, let them be acknowledged as such.'

In fact, of all the great Victorian novelists, Trollope was the readiest to accept the system as he found it. Like Thackeray's his novels move a bit from left to right as he grows older: the early Barsetshire novels are perhaps rather less well-disposed towards the aristocracy in general, and to the Palliser family in particular, than the 'political' series. But his starting point was a good deal less radical than Thackeray's and he did not have to move very far.

Trollope's own background was respectable, but straitened. His father, an unsuccessful lawyer/farmer in continual financial difficulties, was the son of a rector; his mother, also child of a clergyman, eventually became a successful novelist in her own right. He himself had an unhappy and humiliating boyhood at Harrow as a day pupil: 'What right had a wretched farmer's boy, reeking from a dunghill, to sit next to the sons of peers,—or much worse still, next to the sons of big tradesmen who had made their ten thousand a year?' The humiliation did not make him envious and bitter, as it might have done, but gave him a longing for money and position and for all 'the good things' (a favourite phrase of his) that belonged to them. It made him ambitious to grow up 'towards the light, as the trees do'. It spurred him on to stand—unsuccessfully—as a Liberal candidate for Parliament.

There are occasional Dickensian touches in Trollope's work: the aristocratic de Courcys are almost unsympathetic enough to have been created by Dickens and there are some passages of humour or sentiment where he seems to catch at Dickens's manner. He appreciated Dickens's brilliance, but he admired him much less than he did Thackeray and there was certainly less in common between them. Trollope was himself so lacking in revolutionary fervour that, though they sometimes depict social injustice, his novels scarcely touch on class struggle or social oppression.[1] Although a professed Liberal, Trollope was against the introduction of competitive examination for appointment to the civil service. He took up the theme of ecclesiastical abuse, in *The Warden*; but managed to give the impression that his instinctive sympathies were really with the unreformed past. It was in this book that he caricatured Dickens as Mr. Popular Sentiment:

'It is incredible the number of evil practices he has put down: it is to be feared he will soon lack subjects, and that when he has made the working classes comfortable, and got bitter beer put into proper-sized pint bottles, there will be nothing further for him left to do. Mr. Sentiment is certainly a very powerful man, and perhaps not the less so that his good poor people are so very good; his hard rich people so very hard; and the genuinely honest so very honest. Namby-pamby in these days is not thrown away if it be introduced in the proper quarters. Peeresses are no longer interesting, though possessed of every virtue; but a pattern peasant or an immaculate manufacturing hero may talk as much twaddle as one of Mrs. Ratcliffe's heroines, and still be listened to.'

Whatever Trollope's political beliefs, his regard for old family, his passion for fox-hunting, his dislike of stock-jobbing (compare *The Three Clerks* and *The Way We Live Now*), his attachment to English country life, his insistence on political faith and honesty,

---

[1] Daniel Thwaite in *Lady Anna* (set in the 1830s) is strong against social distinctions and regards gentlemen as 'savages' doomed to gradual extinction. But the novel closes with the expectation of his becoming a wiser man.

were all in the authentic Tory tradition and recall the old 'country party' of the squires and parsons.

In almost every book there are one or more examples of a fine, old, conservative, squirearchical family, living on lands which it has owned for generations and making up with honour for any lack of brilliance. The portraits of these Tory families are invariably respectful. The Dales had been squires 'since squires, such as squires are now, were first known in England'. The Greshams 'from time immemorial had been handsome'—broad browed, blue eyed, fair haired. Mr. Thorne of Ullathorne 'counted back his own ancestors to some period long antecedent to the Conquest'. In spite of some gentle ridicule of Mr. and Miss Thorne's genealogical enthusiasm Trollope approves of them: 'Such, we believe, are the inhabitants of many an English country home. May it be long before their number diminishes.' Frank Greystock's father was 'a fine old Tory of the ancient school': 'There is a large body of such men in England, and, personally, they are the very salt of the nation'. The Fletchers in Herefordshire went back well before Henry VII, while Mrs. Fletcher's ancestors 'had been Welsh kings in the time of the Romans'. Arthur Fletcher had 'just that shape of mouth and chin which such men as Abel Wharton regarded as characteristic of good blood'. One begins to wonder whether England ever contained quite so many old landed families. The nobility may often be *parvenu*; but the gentry is impeccably ancestral.

In his dealings with the higher aristocracy Trollope started with an instinctive—and typically Tory—suspicion of Whig grandeur. The de Courcys and the Proudies are Whigs; so is the old Duke of Omnium, who 'was very willing that the Queen should be queen so long as he was allowed to be Duke of Omnium. . . Their revenues were about the same, with the exception, that the duke's were his own, and he could do what he liked with them'. It seems clear enough, in *Doctor Thorne*, that Trollope shares Frank Gresham's disapproval of the Duke's aloof behaviour at his 'collection' at Gatherum Castle, when he gives his undistinguished neighbours the best of food and drink but as little of his company as he can manage. 'There is no one . . . so inclined to high domestic despotism as your thorough-going consistent old Whig.'

But Trollope gradually warms to the Palliser family and, after keeping them in the wings in the Barsetshire novels, brings them on to the centre of the stage in the 'political' series. Even the old Duke's aloofness becomes a kind of merit. By the time of *Phineas Finn* it appears that he is generally regarded 'with an almost reverential awe'. Trollope has no great respect for him himself: he is not a particularly estimable man; he has done no work for the country and his private life is not at all exemplary. But he 'had not been common in the eyes of the people. He had contrived to envelope himself in something of the ancient mystery of wealth and rank.' The clever Madame Goesler says of him in *Phineas Redux*:

'I have an idea that such characters as those of the present Duke are necessary to the maintenance of a great aristocracy. He has had the power of making the world believe in him simply because he has been rich and a duke. His nephew, when he comes to the title, will never receive a tithe of the respect that has been paid to this old faineant.'

Barrington Erle in *Phineas Redux* is an aristocratic Whig. He tells Phineas that he believes 'in the patriotism of certain families. I believe that the Mildmays, FitzHowards and Pallisers have for some centuries brought up their children to regard the well-being of their country as their highest personal interest, and that such teaching has been generally efficacious . . . the school in which good training is most practised will, as a rule, turn out the best scholars. In this way I believe in families.'

This passage may not be especially applicable to the old Duke of Omnium, but it does apply to Plantagenet Palliser, who eventually succeeds his uncle in the title. 'Planty Pall', though not a very lively character, was one of Trollope's heroes. Writing of the Pallisers in his *Autobiography* he said:

'In these personages and their friends . . . I have endeavoured to depict the faults and frailties and vices,—as also the virtues, the graces, and the strength of our highest classes; and if I have not made the strength and virtues predominant over the faults and vices, I have not painted the picture as I intended. Plantagenet Palliser I think to be a very noble gentleman,—such a one as justifies to the nation the seeming anomaly of an hereditary peerage and of primogeniture.'

Thus to Trollope the hereditary principle was a 'seeming anomaly', which could be justified by its results. To Thackeray it was an unjustifiable tradition, which might nevertheless be tolerated as part of the national fabric until more enlightened times should come. Yet both believed in progress towards greater social equality and both regarded themselves as Liberals. Trollope uses the younger of his Dukes of Omnium (finding him in an unusually expansive mood) as a medium for his own social philosophy. The Duke tells Phineas Finn, in *The Prime Minister*, that the Liberal wants to lessen social distances and to bring the coachman and the Duke nearer together—but very gradually and cautiously. 'How can you look at the bowed back and bent legs and abject face of that poor ploughman, who winter and summer has to drag his rheumatic limbs to his work, while you go a-hunting or sit in pride of place among the foremost few of your country, and say that it all is as it ought to be?' 'Equality would be a heaven, if we could attain it.' But it is a dream and all we can work for is 'some nearer approach to equality.'

That these are Trollope's own views is confirmed in his *Autobiography*, where he describes himself as 'an advanced, but still a conservative liberal' and claims that his political convictions 'have never undergone any change'. Inequalities are painful—'we are struck with awe and horror at the misery of many of our brethren' —but they must be recognized as 'the work of God'. The conscientious Conservative is rightly struck by this divine inequality but, unlike the Liberal, he is blind to 'the equally divine diminution of that inequality'. The Liberal's vision of 'a tendency towards equality' is a necessary one, but it needs to be balanced by Conservative safeguards. *Can You Forgive Her?* refers to 'that exquisite combination of conservatism and progress which is her (England's) present strength and best security for the future'.

In *The Duke's Children* the Duke boasts to an American lady: 'Our peerage is being continually recruited from the ranks of the people, and hence it gets its strength. . . . There is no greater mistake than to suppose that inferiority of birth is a barrier to success in this country.' Nevertheless he does not want his daughter to marry a Commoner, although a 'drawing-nearer of the classes' is presented as his great political object. Trollope comments: '. . . there was an inner feeling in his bosom as to his own family, his own nature, his own children, and his own personal self, which was kept altogether apart from his grand political theories.' This would be human; but other passages show that this 'inner feeling' nestled in the Duke's head as well as his bosom. He felt it to be his positive duty to maintain his order intact as a bulwark of the constitution and hence as a guarantee of the right kind of progress. He was like an imperialist convinced that only continued empire can safeguard progress towards independence.

If pressed, Trollope might have condemned the Duke's Whiggish inconsistency; but he notes it with sympathy and, if he felt any disapproval, it was clearly qualified. For that matter there was nothing ruthlessly logical about his own attitude. His novels cannot have given providence much help in gradually diminishing inequality. He says in *The Prime Minister*: 'No doubt we all entertain great respect for those who by their own energies have raised themselves in the world. . . .' But neither the self-made nor their children come very well out of his books. (Miss Dunstable, the heiress of the Barsetshire series, is a sensible and warm-hearted exception.) Mr. Kennedy (*Phineas Finn*), whose father 'had walked into Glasgow as a little boy,—no doubt with the normal half-crown in his breeches pocket', is unsympathetic; so is Mr. Mason of Groby Park (*Orley Farm*) whose father had been a City merchant; so is Mr. Moffatt (*Dr. Thorne*) whose fortune came from tailoring. All have been assimilated by wealth into the upper class; but they do not adorn it. Sir Roger Scatcherd (*Doctor Thorne*), who started journeyman stonemason and later became contractor, Baronet and landed proprietor, is an able and exceptional man. But he drinks; his son is a ghastly failure as a gentleman; and his wife grieves: 'Ah, doctor! people such as us should never meddle with them above us. See what has come of it. . . .'

The hero of Thackeray's *Philip*—though perfectly well aware of the difference between gentlemen and others—is respected for being no respecter of rank. Bertie Stanhope in Trollope's *Barchester Towers* is equally, if not more, un-rank-conscious; but that is because he has no principles at all. Bertie 'had no respect for rank[1]

---

[1] In *The Claverings* Trollope lays down as a commonplace: 'It is well that some respect should be maintained from the low in station towards those who are high, even when no respect has been deserved.'

and no aversion to those below him. He had lived on familiar terms with English peers, German shopkeepers, and Roman priests. All people were nearly alike to him. He was above, or rather below, all prejudices.' He had no social, just as he had no moral, sense.

Trollope writes in his *Autobiography*, apropos of the new system of examination for the civil service: 'There are places in life which can hardly be well filled except by "Gentlemen" . . . It may be that the son of the butcher in the village shall become as well fitted for employments requiring gentle culture as the son of the parson . . . but the chances are greatly in favour of the parson's son. The gates of the one class should be open to the other; but neither to one class or to the other can good be done by declaring that there are no gates, no barrier, no difference.' He was not impatient to abolish, or even lessen, the difference. It was more important that the standards of gentlemanly conduct should be perpetuated. He wanted to alleviate economic misery; but class barriers, as such, were not repugnant to him.

Yet in spite of his Tory instincts, Trollope was enough of a Liberal to avoid the more extreme forms of blood-worship. Mary Thorne is untainted by her working class mother—whom admittedly she never knew—while Dr. Thorne is mildly criticized for his excessive pride of family:

'His father had been a Thorne, and his mother a Thorold. There was no better blood to be had in England. It was in the possession of such properties as these that he condescended to rejoice; this man, with a man's heart, a man's courage, and a man's humanity! Other doctors round the county had ditch-water in their veins; he could boast of a pure ichor, to which that of the great Omnium family was but a muddy puddle.'

Dr. Thorne's cousin, Wilfrid Thorne of Ullathorne, also comes in for some gentle irony in *Barchester Towers*. Mr. Thorne did not look down on *parvenus*, but he 'looked on them as great millionaires are apt to look on those who have small incomes; as men who have Sophocles at their fingers' ends regard those who know nothing of Greek . . . nothing could atone for the loss of good blood; nothing could neutralise its good effects. Few indeed were now possessed of it, but the possession was on that account the more precious.'

Mary Thorne, when contemplating marriage with Frank Gresham of Greshamsbury, comes to wonder: 'What, after all, was this blood of which she had taught herself to think so much? . . . Could it be well that she should sacrifice the happiness of two persons to a theoretic love of pure blood?'

Marriage is the acid test of social attitudes and it is not surprising that love between different social ranks should be a central theme of Trollope's novels. Like Thackeray he comes down on the side of the heart. He certainly disapproves of marriages made for ambition, while he is ready to favour seemingly imprudent matches so long as love is present. It was right for Mary Thorne to marry Frank Gresham—though the match was made a good deal easier by her unexpected inheritance of a fortune. In the words of Mr. Gresham senior, 'the undoubted advantages arising from wealth' could be 'taken by the world as atoning for what would otherwise be a *mesalliance.*' It would have been right for poor Augusta Gresham to accept the gentlemanly London solicitor, Mr. Mortimer Gazebee. When repulsed, on grounds of snobbish principle, he makes a perfectly decorous marriage with her social superior, Lady Amelia de Courcy. Major Grantly in the *Last Chronicle of Barset* does well to marry Grace Crawley in spite of her family's poverty and his father's fear that she could not have had a lady-like upbringing. By contrast his sister's grand marriage to Lord Dumbello (later Marquis of Hartletop) is heartless—she has no heart—and estranges her from her family. No insuperable obstacles are seen to an engagement between Mary Wortle and young Lord Carstairs in *Dr. Wortle's School.* All parties except the young Lord himself take to the idea with caution; but after all there was 'no reason why the son of a peer should not marry the daughter of a clergyman'.

Lady Lufton in *Framley Parsonage* is at first more difficult about her son's wish to marry Lucy Robarts:

'Lucy was the sister of a gentleman who by his peculiar position as parish clergyman of Framley was unfitted to be the brother-in-law of the owner of Framley. . . . And then, too, Lucy's education had been so deficient. She had had no one about her in early life accustomed to the ways of,—of what shall I say without making Lady Lufton appear more worldly than she was ? . . . The species of power in young ladies which Lady Lufton most admired was the *vis inertiae* belonging to beautiful and dignified reticence; of this poor Lucy had none. Then, too, she had no fortune, which, though a minor evil, was an evil; and she had no birth, in the high-life sense of the word, which was a greater evil. . . .'

Yet, in the end, Lucy wins the heart of her mother-in-law as well as of her husband.

But there were realistic limits to Trollope's liberalism, even in affairs of the heart. In the late novel, *Marion Fay*, the son and daughter of a relatively radical Marquis both contemplate marrying beneath them; but the daughter's fiancé turns out to be an Italian Duke by birth (though an English Post Office clerk by career) while the Quaker heroine, who is loved by the son, falls into an early decline, and dies. Unequal matches might occasionally prosper, but they were bound to cause worry and their paths should not run too smooth. Above all, the inequality should not be too great. The inferior party, when marrying into the upper classes, must at least have the manners and instincts of a lady or gentleman. Daniel Thwaite, the tailor's son, hardly has these, though the Solicitor-General does not see why, with his means and talents, he should not 'make as good a gentleman as the rest of us'. But, when he marries Lady Anna, he does not really marry into the upper classes because they go to live abroad.

In any case, as the following passage from *The Three Clerks* suggests, a woman might personally find it a shade easier to marry beneath her than a man:

'There are those who boast that a gentleman must always be a gentleman; that a man . . . raises or degrades his wife to the level of his own condition. . . . How a king may fare in such a condition, the author, knowing little of kings, will not pretend to say; nor yet will he offer an opinion whether a lowly match be fatally injurious to a marquess, duke, or earl; but this he will be bold to affirm, that a man from the ordinary ranks of the upper classes, who has had the nurture of a gentleman, prepares for himself a hell on earth in taking a wife from any rank much below his own. . . . She may be endowed with all those moral virtues which should adorn all women, and which, thank God, are common to women in this country; but he will have to endure habits, manners, and ideas, which the close contiguity of married life will force upon his disgusted palate, and which must banish all love. Man by instinct desires in his wife something softer, sweeter, more refined than himself. . . .'

The 'disgusted palate' recalls the aesthetic side to Trollope's moral and social outlook: his regard for what was comely and fitting. Much in his love of Barsetshire was aesthetic; he could never have written so lovingly of ugly industrial towns. With his feeling for traditional order and decency he was really a humane and liberal Conservative, rather than the conservative Liberal he fancied himself to be. Nothing could be more Tory than what he wrote in praise of the landed interest in *Doctor Thorne*:

'England is not yet a commercial country in the sense in which that epithet is used for her; and let us hope that she will not soon become so. She might surely as well be called feudal England, or chivalrous England. . . . She may excel other nations in commerce, but yet it is not that in which she most prides herself, in which she most excels. Merchants as such are not the first men among us; though it perhaps be open, barely open, to a merchant to become one of them. Buying and selling is good and necessary; it is very necessary, and may, possibly, be very good; but it cannot be the noblest work of man; and let us hope that it may not in our time be esteemed the noblest work of an Englishman.'

In *The Way We Live Now*, which attacks commercial and social fraud, Roger Carbury, an honourable and rather old-fashioned country gentleman, is intended to show up the shoddiness of the other characters. Carbury, acknowledging that he likes the country better than the town, says of Suffolk:

'The people are hearty, and radicalism is not quite so rampant as it is elsewhere. The poor people touch their hats, and the rich people think of the poor. There is something left among us of old English habits.'

Sir Harry Hotspur of Humblethwaite, a man of great posses-
sions, would have taught his dead son the lesson of *noblesse oblige*:
he 'had already begun to teach him when the great blow came,
that all this was to be given to him not that he might put it into his
belly, or wear it on his own back, or even spend it as he might list
himself, but that he might do his part in maintaining that order of
gentlehood in England, by which England had become—so
thought Sir Harry—the proudest and the greatest and the justest
of nations.'

So surely thought Trollope—at heart an admirer of quality, not
equality.

*   *   *

Of the novelists discussed in this book only Dickens could be
described, even remotely, as a social revolutionary. Kingsley's
Alton Locke has a strongly radical, but scarcely a revolutionary,
flavour. Thackeray struck a blow or two for the classless society
in the *Book of Snobs*; but he had too much feeling for what he
attacked to hurt it mortally. In any case, even in his more indignant
moments, he hardly seems to have envisaged revolution as going
beyond a loosening of ranks and the replacement of a hereditary
aristocracy by an educated *bourgeoisie*. Dickens himself was not so
much concerned to overhaul the social system as to put right
abuses, to insist that the poor mattered, and to appeal for less
hardness of heart in social relations; his gospel was in essence a
fiercer and more partisan version of Mrs. Gaskell's.

Taken as a whole the novelists used their influence, not on
behalf of classlessness, nor even to promote a different order of
classes, but to urge more humanity and less hypocrisy in class
dealings. Men should avoid arrogance to those beneath and ob-
sequious imitation of those above; they should stick to their
station, their true feelings and their rights; if they rose, they should
do so with dignity and without pretence.

It was, of course, by appealing to the emotions—whether
pathetically or humorously—that the novelists sought to make
their readers conscious of what was due to themselves and to
others. Humour could correct extravagance, while pathos could
melt hearts. Dickens appealed unsparingly to simple emotions, of

an ageless and universal kind. Others went back to the past, or turned to that part of the present in which the past was most alive, to redress the balance of an increasingly competitive society. Disraeli did this self-consciously and rather artificially. The rest were less deliberately nostalgic, but still cherished traditional social ideals to a remarkable extent. They had nothing against old family and little against the inherited pattern of rural life; they respected benevolent and honourable gentlemen and admired pure and gracious ladies. George Eliot might have felt inclined to attack feudalism; but she did not care to reject what was wholesome and pleasant in her childhood memories. Surtees, less divorced from the country, was perhaps less sentimental about it; but his sympathies were in any case with the class of country gentlemen to which he belonged. Trollope (for all his belief in greater eventual equality a powerful champion of the existing order) made no bones that he believed the best of England to be preserved in her country houses.

Perhaps the solidity of the mid-Victorian system was increased by a vague sense that values and power were shifting, that money was becoming more important than land and that the barbarians were beginning to beat at the gates. The apparently tranquil social climate was in fact that of an Indian Summer. A touch of insecurity, whether or not conscious, gave an added savour to the past and its still ample inheritance. In depicting or recalling the virtues of rural life, and traditional standards of social conduct, the novelists may have been seeking a reassurance against social disintegration, as well as an antidote to the ruthlessness of industrial and social competition. But there was, as yet, no trace of panic in this attitude; disintegration was a long way off; for many, perhaps most, novel-readers traditional social standards were the only ones that mattered.

The streak of social orthodoxy running through the work of the Victorian novelists is most obvious in their attachment to what was 'gentlemanly' and 'ladylike'. The vital question of what constituted a 'gentleman' or 'lady' must be asked, even though it was never definitively answered.

6. Ladies and Gentlemen

The previous chapters have already been heavily sprinkled with the words 'lady' and 'gentleman'. One cannot read long in any Victorian novel without coming across them. What did they mean to the novelists and their readers?

To understand the sense (or rather the various senses) in which Victorians used these words, it is not essential to delve deeply into their origins or their pre-Victorian use. But it is probably true that, even for Victorians, they had a vaguely archaic flavour and tended to recall traditional English values. They were of course aristocratic, not democratic, terms; public speeches and conveniences apart, they never became (as they easily might have done) polite euphemisms for 'men' and 'women'. That their use was so frequent, in spite of this, showed the way in which the old, hierarchical, England continued to dominate English society.

An early nineteenth-century street ballad, maudlin with the nostalgia typical of *Young England*, sang of 'a fine old English gentleman, who had an old estate and who kept up his old mansion at a bountiful old rate, with a good old porter to relieve the old poor at his gate!' Even today the word 'gentleman' carries nostalgic echoes and has never quite escaped from its connection with the country gentry. The connection was still strong in the nineteenth century, but already less strong than it had been. Hence the word tended to conjure up an image—usually a flattering image—of past chivalry and liberality.

But at the same time, even in a narrow social sense, living people could turn themselves into ladies and gentlemen—or at least their children or grandchildren could. Since the terms had never denoted an exclusive caste, gentility could be a legitimate, and an attainable, object of ambition. This was of course also true of noble rank; but titles were few and could only be conferred by Queen or Government. A wealthy self-made man could, by his own efforts, choose to 'live like a gentleman' and to bequeath actual gentility to his more or less immediate descendants.

How strong the ambition could be is illustrated by the ex-convict's feeling of proprietorship towards Pip in *Great Expectations*.

He knew that he could never be a gentleman himself; but he had caught Pip young and could taste the joy of creation: '. . . this is the gentleman what I made! The real, genuine one!' Of course, to the very grand, it might not seem so much to be able to call oneself a gentleman. The Duke of Omnium in Trollope's *The Duke's Children* does not think it enough in his son-in-law: 'There is not a clerk in one of our public offices who does not consider himself to be a gentleman. The curate of the parish is a gentleman, and the medical man who comes here from Bradstock. The word is too vague to carry with it any meaning that ought to be serviceable to you in thinking of such a matter.' But his daughter stoutly replies: 'I do not know any other way of dividing people. . . .' Most Victorians thought it a great thing to be on the right side of that dividing line. Thackeray, enthusing about the 'high-bred English lady', thought that duchesses and countesses 'can be but ladies, and no more'. Trollope's Roger Carbury believed that a gentleman born could not be made more of one by a title.

It followed that the words were modern as well as old-fashioned. They had intense contemporary significance; they meant something that was alive and changing, as well as something that was traditional and fixed. The way in which they served the purposes both of continuity and progress was very typical of Victorian society. Their constant use must itself have fostered the social values that they typified. Englishmen thought in these categories because it suited them; but what suited them was in turn shaped by the categories in which, for historical and linguistic reasons, they had been trained to think.

The Victorian gentleman could be so in an *ancestral*, or in a *social*, or in a *moral*, sense. Strictly speaking, in the first sense, the term stood for a man of gentle, but not noble, birth with the right of bearing arms. Many gentlemen in Victorian novels do in fact belong to this class, usually attached to country estates which maintain and express their family fortunes. Without doubt birth gave the surest title to gentility: there was a mystique about it which nothing could wholly destroy. Much as they loved worldly success most Victorians were ready to respect a gentleman by birth, even though he had fallen into obscurity and poverty.

Whether a man of good descent could still be considered a

gentleman, if neither he nor his parents had been educated as gentlefolk, was perhaps another question. Fortunately it did not often arise: either the gentility was forgotten or ambition kept it, genuinely, alive. But, even when poverty and obscurity had been prolonged, a claim to remote, ancestral, gentility was worth asserting by anybody on the make. Gentle birth was widely regarded as conferring an inner grace, bound to reveal itself in mental or physical refinement and capable of being transmitted, almost indefinitely, down the generations.

How ancestral gentility had begun might be scarcely less mysterious than how (if ever) it ended. What first kindled the divine spark? Disraeli and Thackeray loved to show up the recency of titled families and their origins in favour and corruption. But, equally, most Victorian novelists (and Disraeli among them) delighted in stressing how very old some of their ordinary country families were. The difficulty of accounting for ancestral gentility perhaps becomes less pressing the further its origins are pushed back. It is surprising, today, to travel in the fictional countryside of Trollope's novels and find so many mansions occupied by families with established mediaeval, or even Saxon, roots. Major Grantly in the *Last Chronicle of Barset* politely asks about Squire Dale's house, which was built in 1617: 'Your own ancestors were living here before that, I suppose?' 'Well, yes; two or three hundred years before it, I suppose. . . .' There are not many parts of England where such suppositions could safely be made now; and perhaps there could never have been quite as much scope for them as the novelists suggest. Somebody says in Mrs. Gaskell's *Wives and Daughters* '. . . it's a pity when these old Saxon houses vanish off the land', as if 'old Saxon houses' were a regular feature of the social landscape.

There is a remarkable insistence in Victorian novels on the physical attributes of breeding. Mrs. Gaskell's Squire Hamley, though of an 'old Saxon house', is an exception: '. . . here am I' he exclaims 'of as good and as old a descent as any man in England, and I doubt if a stranger, to look at me, would take me for a gentleman, with my red face, great hands and feet, and thick figure, fourteen stone. . . .' But Mr. Irwine in *Adam Bede* shows his blood in his 'finely-cut nostril and upper lip', while Disraeli regarded a short upper lip as a sure proof of old family. Eppie in *Silas Marner* and Esther in *Felix Holt* are, like Oliver Twist, of gentler birth than upbringing; all three have a sort of refinement: Eppie's 'delicate prettiness' is not quite that of a 'common village maiden'. Trollope's Phineas Finn had 'a look of breeding about him which had come to him, no doubt, from the royal Finns of old . . .' To Lord George Germain, in *Is He Popenjoy?*, 'birth and culture' had given 'a look of intellect greater than he possessed'. In the *Vicar of Bullhampton* there is a more cautious reference: the Rev. Frank Fenwick had 'more of breeding in his appearance than his friend, a show of higher blood; though whence comes such show, and how one discerns that appearance, few of us can tell.' But the tone of certainty returns in *An Old Man's Love*:

'How many a face, otherwise lovely to look upon, is made mean and comparatively base, either by the lengthening or the shortening of the chin! That absolute perfection which Miss Lawrie owned, we do not perhaps often meet. But when found, I confess that nothing to me gives so sure an evidence of true blood and good-breeding.'

The novelists seldom sought to rationalize the mystique of 'good family'. Most of their readers probably took for granted that it had intrinsic value and was to be revered like revealed truth. But there are passages in Trollope which suggest that he had a theory of 'blood'. In *Marion Fay* he makes a character exclaim: 'You Radicals may say what you please, but silk purses don't get made out of sows' ears. Nobody stands up for blood less than I do; but, by George, it always shows itself.' In *Sir Harry Hotspur of Humblethwaite* Trollope writes as if, though blood could not do everything for a man, it could do for him what it could for a hunter or a racehorse:

'Noblesse oblige. High position will demand, and will often exact, high work. But that rule holds as good with a Buonaparte as with a Bourbon, with a Cromwell as with a Stewart; and succeeds as often and fails as often with the low born as with the high. And good blood too will have its effect,—physical for the most part,— and will produce bottom, lasting courage, that capacity of carrying through the mud to which Sir Harry was wont to allude; but good blood will bring no man back to honesty. The two things together, no doubt, assist in producing the highest order of self-denying man.'

Mary Thorne does not necessarily speak for Trollope, because her uncle, who has brought her up, is exaggeratedly proud of his descent. But, to the questions: what makes a gentleman? what makes a gentlewoman? what is the inner reality of rank?, she seems to answer as Trollope might have done: 'Absolute, intrinsic, acknowledged, individual merit must give it to its possessor, let him be whom, and what, and whence he might . . . Beyond this it could be had but by inheritance, received as it were second-hand, or twenty-second hand.'

Here is one rationalization, though perhaps not a very convincing one until men are mated as scientifically as race-horses. (Was it blood, or pride, that made for gentlemanly courage?) Another, less controversial, was hinted by the novelists, when they noted— as they often did—how awareness of belonging to a good family, combined with social and educational polish, made for self-assurance and easy manners. Even the critical Thackeray notes this ease of manner as a characteristic of 'the great world'.

In a wider and less technical sense of the word, of course, it was not necessary to belong to the landed gentry to be a gentleman. A peer could be (could hardly not be) a gentleman in the ordinary, *social*, sense of the term. So could any educated man, more or less, whose father, for one reason or another, had been accepted as a gentleman. Even men whose fathers had not been gentlemanly at all could sometimes qualify. A clever adventurer, or the rich son of a self-made man, might pass muster by associating with gentlemen and acquiring their habits—though it needed considerable social skill to do this without a good stock of money and education. Public schools played a less central role in producing gentlemen than subsequently; but they could make a substantial difference. Sir William Patterson, in Trollope's *Lady Anna*, had several qualifications to be a gentleman; not the least was that he 'had been at a public school, and had lived all his days with people of the right sort'.

Manners and conduct went far towards making a gentleman; and to acquire these a good education was usually necessary. The more uncertain the gentility, the more essential it was to behave properly. Men who were born gentle might be accused of not behaving like gentlemen; but it would be going rather far to describe them as not being gentlemen at all.

It was widely accepted that, whatever their birth, barristers, Anglican clergymen and officers in the armed services could become gentlemen, through their professions, provided that they spoke and behaved more or less as gentlemen should. Conversely there was work that a gentleman could not touch without being defiled. Miss Marrable in *The Vicar of Bullhampton* (1870) had strong, old-fashioned, views on the subject and, being of good family herself, 'thought a good deal about blood':

'She was one of those ladies,—now few in number,—who within their heart of hearts conceive that money gives no title to social distinction. . . . She had an idea that the son of a gentleman, if he intended to maintain his rank as a gentleman, should earn his income as a clergyman, or as a barrister, or as a soldier, or as a sailor. . . . She would not absolutely say that a physician was not a gentleman, or even a surgeon; but she would never allow to physic the same absolute privileges which, in her eyes, belonged to law and the church. There might also possibly be a doubt about the Civil Service and Civil Engineering; but she had no doubt whatever that when a man touched trade or commerce in any way he was doing that which was not the work of a gentleman. He might be very respectable, and it might be very necessary that he should do it; but brewers, bankers, and merchants, were not gentlemen, and the world, according to Miss Marrable's theory, was going astray, because people were forgetting their landmarks.'

For ladies, as well as for gentlemen, birth was the most dependable touchstone. Unlike gentlemen, they could not qualify through a profession. Almost the only profession available to the ladylike was that of a governess; impoverished ladies might be governesses but, if they were not ladies, being governesses would not of course make them so. Education would help—though more often and effectively in a well-bred home than in a school. Where aspiring ladies had the advantage over men was that, while no man could become a gentleman simply through marrying above him, a woman would take her husband's rank and a gentleman would insist on his wife being treated as a lady. A young and adaptable gosling could hope to spread out as a swan.

There was of course a fairly wide area of dispute over the right to claim these titles. The Dean of Brotherton, in *Is He Popenjoy?*, was a sensible man and had the position and manners of a gentleman. But his father had kept a livery stable and sensitive nostrils still caught a faint whiff of the stable yard. Eton and Cambridge failed to make a gentleman of young Scatcherd in *Dr. Thorne*. The whole moral of the sub-plot of *The Prime Minister* is that Ferdinand Lopez, who appears to be a gentleman in his manner, but whose gentlemanliness cannot be certified, since his background is unknown, turns out to behave quite otherwise than a gentleman should. Nobody believes Lopez to be well-born and he is employed in the City 'on business which does not of itself give such a warrant of position as is supposed to be afforded by the bar and the church, by military services and by physic'. Yet, at the beginning of the book, he is admitted on all sides to be a gentleman. Trollope comments:

'Johnson says that any other derivation of this difficult word than that which causes it to signify "a man of ancestry" is whimsical. There are many, who in defining the term for their own use, still adhere to Johnson's dictum;—but they adhere to it with certain unexpressed allowances for possible exceptions.'

Lopez is distasteful to his father-in-law 'as being without those far-reaching fibres and roots by which he thought that the stability of a human tree should be assured'. But his father-in-law was old-fashioned and thought that 'a man doesn't often become a gentleman in the first generation'. In spite of her father's doubts Emily Wharton marries Lopez, believing the gift of 'gentle blood and of gentle nurture' to be 'a weak, spiritless quality'. Yet she comes to acknowledge this as a mistake. It is brought in on her, painfully, that Arthur Fletcher has a 'peculiar gift, or grace, or acquirement' lacking in her husband: '. . . she had commenced to learn what it was that her father had meant when he spoke of the pleasure of living with gentlemen. Arthur Fletcher . . . would not have entertained the suspicions which her husband had expressed.'

Lopez goes from bad to worse and the final verdict on him is severe: 'In a sense he was what is called a gentleman. He knew how to speak, and how to look, how to use a knife and fork, how to dress himself, and how to walk. But he had not the faintest notion of the feelings of a gentleman.'

Yet, in the same book, Emily makes a friend of the uneducated Mrs. Parker and learns to value her 'practical good sense and proper feeling': 'The lady who was a lady had begun to feel that in the troubles of life she might find a much less satisfactory companion than the lady who was not a lady.' Why was it so inevitable that the not-quite-gentleman Lopez should lack the 'practical good sense and proper feeling' of the un-lady-like Mrs. Parker?

There are several references in Trollope to the difficulty of defining gentility. Johnny Eames says in *The Last Chronicle of Barset*: 'I can't define a gentleman, even in my own mind.' But, if it cannot be defined, there seems to be no problem about detecting it. In *He Knew He Was Right* it is described as 'that thing, so impossible of definition, and so capable of recognition'. The low-church Mr. Prong in *Rachel Ray* was

'deficient in one vital qualification for a clergyman of the Church of England; he was not a gentleman. May I not call it a necessary qualification for a clergyman of any church? He was not a gentleman. I do not mean to say that he was a thief or a liar; nor do I mean hereby to complain that he picked his teeth with his fork and misplaced his "h's". I am by no means prepared to define what I do mean—thinking, however, that most men and most women will understand me . . . his efficiency for clerical purposes was marred altogether, among high and low, by his misfortune in this respect. . . . They who have not good coats themselves have the keenest eyes for the coats of their better-clad neighbours. As it is with coats, so it is with that which we call gentility. It is caught at a word, it is seen at a glance, it is appreciated unconsciously at a touch by those who have none of it themselves. It is the greatest of all aids to the doctor, the lawyer, the member of Parliament— though in that position a man may perhaps prosper without it,— and to the statesman; but to the clergyman it is a vital necessity.'

Here was a state of grace, then, that could be recognized by the elect and non-elect alike. Ladies and gentlemen would certainly be indignant if their own powers of recognition were questioned. In *The Belton Estate* Captain Aylmer, offended by the brusque behaviour of his rival, Will Belton, asks Clara Amedroz:

' "Do you really think that he has conducted himself today like a gentleman?"

"I know that he is a gentleman", said Clara.

"I must confess I have no reason for supposing him to be so but your assurance."

"And I hope that is sufficient, Frederic." '

But Trollope thought that some of the shrewdest judges were to be found below the gentility line. The servants at Buston, in *Mr. Scarborough's Family*, 'had their own ideas of a lady and gentleman, which, as in all such cases, was perfectly correct. They knew the squire to be a fool, but they believed him to be a gentleman. They heard that Miss Thoroughbung was a clever woman, but they did not believe her to be a lady.' The grooms in Barchester knew Mr. Crawley to be a gentleman, although he was to be tried as a thief and his boots were cracked and his clothes ragged:

'Nobody doubted it; not even they who thought he had stolen the money. Mr. Robarts himself was certain of it, and told himself that he knew it by evidences which his own education made clear to him. But how was it that the grooms knew it? For my part I think that there are no better judges of the article than the grooms.'

Surtees has a rather more cynical view of servants as judges of gentility. In *Ask Mamma* Billy Pringle's mother, when a lady's maid, had been happy to serve Lady Delacey, who never demeaned herself by wearing the same gloves or ball-shoes twice or gave to the nurse what she should have given the lady's maid: 'She was a real lady, in the proper acceptation of the term.' Similarly, in *Mr. Sponge's Sporting Tour*, a gamekeeper speaks of a former master: '. . . a *real* gentleman now, if you like—free, open-handed gentleman—none of your close shavin', cheese-parin' sort of gentlemen, or imitation gentlemen, as I calls them, but a man who knew what was due to good servants and gave them it.'

All the novelists furnished hints as to how ladies and gentlemen, in the social sense, might be recognized. Caroline Helstone, in *Shirley*, was William Farren's ideal of a lady: 'Her gentle mien, step, gestures, her grace of person and attire, moved some artist-fibres about his peasant heart.' In *Wives and Daughters* Mollie Gibson is ashamed, after her visit to the Hamleys, at noticing 'the coarser and louder tones' in which the Miss Brownings spoke, 'the provincialism of their pronunciation, the absence of interest in things, and their greediness of details about persons.' Miss Nancy in *Silas Marner*, badly informed as she was, 'had the essential attributes of a lady—high veracity, delicate honour in her dealings, deference to others, and refined personal habits. . . .' Alton Locke, admiring Eleanor Staunton, finds the grace with which her plain dress is arranged enough 'to proclaim her a fine lady; by which term I wish to express the result of that perfect education in taste and manner, down to every gesture, which Heaven forbid that I, professing to be a poet, should under-value. . . .' Clive Newcome tells his father that Aunt Hobson is not *'comme il faut'*: '. . . one can't help seeing the difference. It isn't rank and that; only somehow there are some women ladies and some not. . . . Aunt Ann is different, and it seems as if what she says is more natural; and though she has funny ways of her own too, yet somehow she looks grander. . . .'

Grace, taste, honour, personal refinement, lack of affectation: *mutatis mutandis* these were supposed to be attributes of gentlemen, too. The narrator's father, in *My Lady Ludlow*, was 'too true a gentleman to feel false shame'. In *Ruth* Mr. Donne makes an immediate impact on the provincial Bradshaw household; Mr. Bradshaw felt in less than half an hour

'the quiet but incontestable difference of rank and standard that there was, in every respect, between his guest and his own family. It was not through any circumstance so palpable, and possibly accidental, as the bringing down a servant. . . It was nothing like this; it was something indescribable—a quiet being at ease, and expecting every one else to be so—an attention to women, which was so habitual as to be unconsciously exercised . . . a happy choice of simple and expressive words, some of which it must be confessed were slang, but fashionable slang, and that makes all the difference—a measured, graceful way of utterance, with a style of pronunciation quite different to that of Eccleston.'

Surtees, in *Ask Mamma*, finds that the only infallible rule is that 'the man who is always talking about being a gentleman never is one.' However, he notes that Billy's trouble was that, on examination, he appeared 'painfully gentlemanly'; there was too much 'nervous twitching, and jerking, and feeling, as if he was wondering what people were thinking or saying of him.' Mr. Sponge has the same trouble: his 'commanding appearance was rather marred by a jerky, twitchy, uneasy sort of air that too plainly showed he was not the natural, or what the lower orders call the *real* gentleman. Not that Sponge was shy. Far from it.' Nevertheless the Jawleyfords are quite ready to be taken in by him, though Miss Jawleyford has her doubts when she sees him staring and blurting and kicking his legs about.

Chivalry towards women, or at least towards ladies, was of course one gentlemanly duty. Lizzie Hexham says to Eugene Wrayburn in *Our Mutual Friend*:

'If you feel towards me, in one particular, as you might if I was a lady, give me the full claims of a lady upon your generous behaviour. I am removed from you and your family by being a working girl. How true a gentleman to be as considerate of me as if I was removed by being a Queen!'

Another supposed characteristic was self-control. Mr. Bucket, the detective, tells Sir Leicester Dedlock in *Bleak House*: '. . . you are a gentleman; and I know what a gentleman is, and what a gentleman is capable of. A gentleman can bear a shock, when it must come, boldly and steadily . . . you naturally think of your family.'

Kingsley's working-class heroes are painfully aware of gentility. Alton Locke believed that, in the higher ranks, a difference in income implied none in education and manners and that even a poor gentleman was a fit companion for dukes and princes. Tregarva, in *Yeast*, appealed to Lancelot:

'. . . look at the difference between yourself and me. When you've lost all you have, and seven times more, you're still a gentleman. No man can take that from you . . . suppose you had loved a pious and a beautiful lady, and among all your worship of her, and your awe of her, had felt that . . . you could become her comforter, and her pride, and her joy, if it wasn't for that accursed gulf that men had put between you, that you were no gentleman; that you didn't know how to walk, and how to pronounce, and when to speak, and when to be silent, not even how to handle your own knife and fork without disgusting her, or how to keep your own body clean and sweet. . . .'

Colonel Newcome, who liked to be 'in the company of gentlemen', no doubt took personal cleanliness and proper table manners for granted; if he thought Sir Roger de Coverley, Sir Charles Grandison and Don Quixote 'the finest gentlemen in the world', it was because they satisfied his ideas of innocence and honour. His creator, inveighing against George IV in the *Book of Snobs*, invoked a still more comprehensive ideal:

'What is it to be a gentleman? Is it to be honest, to be gentle, to be generous, to be brave, to be wise, and, possessing all these qualities, to exercise them in the most graceful outward manner? Ought a gentleman to be a loyal son, a true husband, and honest father? Ought his life to be decent—his bills to be paid—his tastes to be high and elegant—his aims in life lofty and noble?'

But this verges on the moral, rather than the social, sense of the term. Not everybody associated the grander forms of social gentility with morality. 'To the Rector' (in *Daniel Deronda*) 'whose father (nobody would have suspected it, and nobody was told) had risen to be a provincial corn-dealer, aristocratic heirship resembled regal heirship in excepting its possessor from the ordinary standard of moral judgements. . . .' In spite of her own extremely strict principles Lady Macleod, in *Can You Forgive Her?*, 'could almost worship a youthful marquis, though he lived a life that would disgrace a heathen among heathens'.

Nevertheless, as we have already seen, the terms 'lady' and 'gentleman', even in their social sense, conveyed notions of virtue, as well as of grace. Young aristocrats might be permitted, and even expected, to live less soberly than the respectable middle-class; but they were not admired (for instance) for cheating at cards or showing physical cowardice. At a lower level of fashion gentlemen could not afford to disregard ordinary moral rules, though the habits of genteel society were not compatible with rigid austerity.

The special virtues of gentility—honour, truth, courage, forbearance towards the defenceless—derived from the mediaeval ideal of chivalry and were of course particularly apt to a military class. Politics, or blood sports, still provided some scope for the warlike instincts of the gentry. But social amenity had had its softening influence and many Victorian gentlemen lived lives that were entirely peaceable. They strove to be 'gentle' in more than one sense—perhaps unconsciously influenced by the vagary of language which had connected two ideals.

At any rate gentleness towards inferiors, if not always practised, was part of the chivalric code and of the gentleman's image. Becky Sharp claimed to be better treated by the Crawleys, as a 'gentleman's family—good old English stock' than by City people. Mrs. Gale in *Shirley* resented the three young curates whom she was obliged to feed:

'they treat her with less than civility, just because she doesn't keep a servant, but does the work of the house herself, as her mother did afore her . . . and by that very token Mrs. Gale does not believe one of them to be a real gentleman, or come of gentle kin. "The old parsons is worth the whole lump of college lads: they know what belongs to good manners, and is kind to high and low."'

Whatever the actual behaviour of ladies and gentlemen, the extent to which the terms were revered is confirmed by the rareness with which, in Victorian novels, they are used in a pejorative sense. Mrs. Gaskell's John Barton is against 'the gentlefolk'; he does not want his daughter to be 'a do-nothing lady, worrying shopmen all morning, and screeching at her pianny all afternoon, and going to bed without having done a good turn to any one of God's creatures but herself.' It could be 'seen with half an eye' that Harthouse, in *Hard Times*, 'was a thorough gentleman, made to the model of the time; weary of everything, and putting no more faith in anything than Lucifer'. Poor Mrs. Burton bursts out against Henry Clavering in *The Claverings*: 'He is to be allowed to be dishonest to my girl because he is a gentleman! I wish there was no such thing as a gentleman—so I do. Perhaps there would be more honest men, then.'

But these are isolated instances; Mrs. Burton is a worried mother and John Barton an embittered man. A more penetrating and revealing passage occurs in *North and South* in a conversation between Mr. Thornton, the manufacturer, and Margaret Hale. The former says:

' "A man is to me a higher and completer being than a gentleman."

"What do you mean?" asked Margaret. "We must understand the words differently."

"I take it that 'gentleman' is a term that only describes a person in his relation to others; but when we speak of him as 'a man', we consider him not merely with regard to his fellow-men, but in relation to himself—to life—to time—to eternity. A castaway, lonely as Robinson Crusoe—a prisoner immured in a dungeon for life—nay, even a saint in Patmos, has his endurance, his strength, his faith, best described by being spoken of as 'a man'. I am rather weary of this word 'gentlemanly'; which seems to me to be often inappropriately used, and often, too, with such exaggerated distortion of meaning, while the full simplicity of the noun 'man', and the adjective 'manly' are unacknowledged—that I am inclined to class it with the cant of the day." '

Mr. Thornton was, of course, quite right. 'Gentlemanly' was an overworked word and there was a good deal of cant about its use. He was also right in pointing out that the social sense of the word (already sufficiently stretched) was only really applicable to external virtues, capable of being displayed in, and perceived by, society. But, whatever a purist might urge, the ideals of 'the perfect lady' and 'the perfect gentleman' had become so prized that they could be, and were, made to embrace almost every type of virtue. It was gentlemanly to be proud and gentlemanly to be meek; it was gentlemanly to be everything that a Victorian thought it right to be. The novelists themselves were among the chief exponents of the third, *moral* sense of the words 'lady' and 'gentleman'. In this sense a man of any class might be a gentleman, or a woman of any class a lady.

Charlotte Brontë uses the words without any direct class reference in *Shirley*, when she exclaims: 'Taken as they ought to be, the majority of the lads and lasses of the West Riding are gentlemen and ladies, every inch of them.' But this is not far from the social sense of the terms, since she has good manners, rather than morals, in mind. When Jem regards Mary Barton, who is certainly not a lady by birth or breeding, as 'a lady by right of nature . . . in movement, grace and spirit', he is evidently thinking of moral, as well as social, refinement. The same fusion of ideas appears in a diary kept by Mrs. Gaskell: 'I think it is Dekker who speaks of our Saviour as "the first true gentleman that ever lived". We may choose to be shocked at the freedom of expression used by the old dramatist: but is it not true? Is not Christianity at the very core of the heart of all gracious courtesy?'

The Duchess in *Coningsby* was perhaps an example of what Mrs. Gaskell had in mind. She was 'distinguished by that perfect good breeding which is the result of nature, and not of education: for it may be found in a cottage, and may be missed in a palace. 'Tis a genial regard for the feelings of others that springs from an absence of selfishness'.

As might be expected, Trollope hesitated to talk of 'ladies' and 'gentlemen' outside the class in which they were properly found. But Mrs. Brattle, the miller's wife in *The Vicar of Bullhampton*, 'was a modest, pure, high-minded woman,—whom we will not call a lady, because of her position in life, and because she darned stockings in a kitchen. In all other respects she deserved the name.' Mrs. Brattle was 'one of those loving, patient, self-denying, almost heavenly human beings, one or two of whom may come across one's path, and who, when found, are generally found in that sphere of life to which this woman belonged. Among the rich there is that difficulty of the needle's eye; among the poor there is the difficulty of the hardness of their lives.'

Writing of Amelia and Dobbin in *Vanity Fair* Thackeray defines gentility in terms that are almost entirely moral. Amelia's 'heart was so pure' and her 'bearing was so meek and humble, that she could not but needs be a true lady. She busied herself in gentle offices and quiet duties; if she never said brilliant things, she never spoke or thought unkind ones; guileless and artless, loving and pure, indeed how could our poor little Amelia be other than a real gentlewoman!' As to gentlemen:

'Which of us can point out many such in his circle—men whose aims are generous, whose truth is constant, and not only constant in its kind but elevated in its degree; whose want of meanness makes them simple: who can look the world honestly in the face with an equal manly sympathy for the great and the small? We all know a hundred whose coats are very well made, and a score who have excellent manners, and one or two happy beings who are what they call in the inner circles, and have shot into the very centre and bull's-eye of the fashion: but of gentlemen how many?'

Yet Thackeray's ideal of gentlemanly perfection, however moral, was not complete without some outward grace or dignity, some height or breadth of aim, that only education could cultivate. It is Dickens who colours the ideal with the least tincture of class.

In *Our Mutual Friend* old Betty Higsden says to kind Mrs. Boffin, who tells her frankly that she 'wasn't born a lady any more than you': 'It seems to me that you were born a lady, and a true one, or there never was a lady born.' Both the plebeian Ham, in *David Copperfield*, and the well-connected Twemlow, in *Our Mutual Friend*, have 'the soul of a gentleman'. Ham treats Emily with gentlemanly chivalry, while Steerforth, a gentleman, betrays her. Sir Leicester Dedlock behaves like the gentleman he is in forgiving his wife; but, lest we should see anything symbolic in his conduct, we are told that it was 'simply honourable, manly and true. Nothing less worthy can be seen through the lustre of such qualities in the commonest mechanic, nothing less worthy can be seen in the best-born gentleman. In such a light both aspire alike, both rise alike, both children of the dust shine equally.'

Great Expectations is an essay in this theme. Pip, born in a smithy, is educated as a gentleman by an unknown benefactor, who turns out to be an ex-convict. He himself conceives the wish to become a gentleman, as a boy, when Estella's contempt for his thick boots, coarse hands and habit of calling Knaves Jacks, makes him feel common. He gets some tactful lessons in table manners from Herbert Pocket and, technically, he does not seem to have too much difficulty in acquiring the necessary polish. Yet all along he feels a suppressed shame at abandoning his childhood friends; in the end the real nobility of Joe Gargery, the blacksmith, together with the discovery of how his education had been financed, makes him feel the tawdriness of his ambition.

Earlier in the book Herbert tells Pip that, according to his (Herbert's) father, 'no man who was not a true gentleman at heart, ever was, since the world began, a true gentleman in manner. He says, no varnish can hide the grain of the wood; and that the more varnish you put on, the more the grain will express itself.' Dickens certainly meant his story to convey that, however unvarnished, Joe Gargery was 'a true gentleman at heart'. Varnish on sound wood might be all very well; but it was the wood that mattered, not the varnish.

The various uses of the words 'gentleman' and 'lady' were liable to cause a good deal of ambiguity, even confusion. Novelists would sometimes go to considerable lengths to make their meaning clear. 'She was simply, almost coarsely dressed' (this is from *Yeast*) 'but a glance told him that she was a lady, by the courtesy of man as well as by the will of God'. In *The Small House at Allington* Trollope felt obliged to insist that Mrs. Dale (although 'her grandfather had been almost nobody') was 'a lady, inwards and outwards, from the crown of her head to the soles of her feet, in head, in heart, and in mind, a lady by education and a lady by nature, a lady also by birth, in spite of that deficiency respecting her grandfather. . . .'

To expect a man to be a complete gentleman in every sense of the word was asking a good deal of human nature. Dolly Grey in *Mr. Scarborough's Family* was unlikely to marry because she expected her husband to qualify as a gentleman in all senses of the word,—ancestral, social and moral—and she did not know many men who did. Objecting to Mr. Barry as a suitor, she asks her father:

'What right has he to be a gentleman? Who was his father and who was his mother? Of what kind were his nursery belongings?

He has become an attorney, and so have you. But has there been anyone to whisper to him among his teachings that in that profession, as in all others, there should be a sense of high honour to guide him? . . . And in the daily intercourse of life would he satisfy what you call my fastidiousness?'

The different meanings given to the words had an important social result. Their usage in a purely moral sense helped to correct class bias. Yet, even if the novel-reader got the impression that the truest ladies and gentlemen were to be found in the lower classes (uncorrupted by wealth, ambition and dissipation), he was still likely to picture them as treading—more firmly than their betters— in their betters' footsteps. However much gentility might be proposed as an ideal for all humanity, it could never be entirely divested of its class associations; there were unmistakable social subtones even in the moral sense of the term. In pursuing a gentlemanly ideal, or feeling that they ought to pursue it, the middle and lower classes were following a fashion set from on high—just as they did when they learned to turn up the bottoms of their trousers, or to grow their whiskers long. A working-class 'gentleman' might be one of 'nature's aristocrats'; but even to regard him in that light tended to separate him from his fellows. Still more was this so if he consciously modelled himself on an aristocratic ideal. The popular use of these words encouraged the lower orders to play cricket, instead of some rougher game of their own.

Conversely, when the words were used in a social sense, they inevitably carried moral subtones. Everybody knew that those who belonged to the class of ladies and gentlemen were not always all that they should be; but everybody also knew that there was something that they ought to be and sometimes were. 'A real gentleman'; 'a lady born and bred'; 'an officer and a gentleman': the frequency of such phrases both conferred a prestige on the upper classes and gave them some stimulus to behave as they were expected to do.

All of this, naturally, had its good side. In many ways it raised the tone of English life and it certainly made for social continuity and stability. But it tended to leave the lower classes without moral defences of their own; their hope was to better themselves individually—by following an essentially aristocratic code—rather than to raise their common condition. Perhaps, after all, George Eliot was the most revolutionary of the novelists when she insisted on Felix Holt staying true to his class.[1]

None of these effects would have been possible if the aristocratic class had been fixed and separate: in that case imitation must have been discouraged and ascent impracticable. The appeal of gentility was as widespread as it was, because every ambitious man could (if he wished) imagine that he carried a gentleman's stick in his knapsack—at least for his son, if not for himself. At the same time those who had no urge or ability to climb could feel that their superiors were better-bred versions of themselves, rather than totally different beings.

Wealth of course imposed social differences as well as gentility; but, although increasingly powerful throughout the nineteenth century, it was still a subordinate principle in English society, at least outside the main centres of industry. On the whole the wealthy were yet more eager to become genteel, than the genteel to become wealthy. However, where wealth was the main standard, different social values—less tied in time and place to Victorian England and of less absorbing interest to the novelists—tended to apply.

For good or ill the notion of gentility made a powerful contribution to English snobbery. Its effect might be democratic in the higher ranks of society, since it set a standard which in some ways limited the authority of titled rank. A peer, taking pride in being a gentleman, might conform to the prejudices of a circle wider than his own order. But, lower down in the social scale, the preoccupation with gentility involved endless petty assumptions of superiority and inferiority, breeding a habit of snobbish classification which many Englishmen disliked—but few could avoid.

Since there was no final arbiter or means of identification,

[1] In this George Eliot followed Samuel Smiles, author of *Self-Help*, who told an audience of Leeds working men in the middle forties:—'The education of the working classes is to be regarded, in its highest aspect, not as a means of raising up a few clever and talented men into a higher rank of life, but of elevating and improving the whole class—of raising the entire condition of the working man.' Smiles did not want his self-made men to become gentlemen except in the most moral sense of the term. But in practice self-help was liable to lead to social gentility, sooner or later. Cf. Chapter Five of *Victorian People* by Professor Asa Briggs.

there could be no single, infallible, way of telling whether a man was a gentleman or not. There were well-established aids to recognition; but they could often be misleading. Sometimes, of course, there was no room for doubt. A man could scarcely be a gentleman in the social sense if he spoke with a Cockney accent; nor could anybody question the basic gentility of a landed man of fortune, education and old family. But there were many people betwixt and between; plebeian behaviour could be found in high places, while bounders could put on convincing performances. (In any case—as with the English language—a great deal was left to individual taste.)

Consequently the detection of ladies and gentlemen became something of a national pastime, governed by elaborate, unspoken, conventions not necessarily shared by all the players. Much energy and ingenuity were devoted to this confusing sport. Two Englishmen, meeting as strangers, would prowl discreetly round each other, not satisfied until they had got each other 'placed'. The conversational mists, half-lights, and sudden illuminations were characteristic of our perplexing climate and of the subtly important, though never absolute, distinctions that pervaded our society.

7. That Gothic Society

'Let us get her last curtsey from her as she stands here upon the English shore. When she gets into the Australian woods her back won't bend except to her labour; or, if it do, from old habit and the reminiscence of the old country, do you suppose her children will be like that timid creature before you? They will know nothing of that Gothic society, with its ranks and hierarchies, its cumbrous ceremonies, its glittering antique paraphernalia, in which we have been educated; in which rich and poor still acquiesce, and which multitudes of both still admire: far removed from these old-world traditions, they will be bred up in the midst of plenty, freedom, manly brotherhood.' (Thackeray: from *Waiting at the Station*: 1847)

The emphasis in the last chapter has been upon the stability of nineteenth-century English society, upon its deferential character, upon its respect for tradition and gentility. Those are in fact the characteristics on which—consciously or unconsciously, in criticism or approval—the Victorian novelists most insisted. The cautiously revolutionary tone of some of the earlier novels soon faded into the conservatism, or acquiescence, of the middle years of the century. This is partly Trollope's doing. If he had written less, or less realistically, or if he had stopped writing sooner, the impression of stability and continuity might be less overwhelming. But, even if he had not written at all, social deference would still be a major theme of Victorian fiction.

An economic or political historian could present Victorian society in a different light. Change and turbulence could be placed in sharper relief than order and complacency. The energies of aspiring individuals, the struggles of competing classes, could be made to look more important than the traditional social framework which they had to master or subvert.

A sense of dynamic change, of great things to come or great dangers to be avoided, is not lacking in the earlier novels of the period. The hero of Lytton's *Ernest Maltravers* (1837) strikes an apolcalyptic note when he compares the last days of the Roman Republic with his own times:

'. . . a *coup d'oeil* of their social state might convey to us a general notion of our own. Their system, like ours—a vast aristocracy heaved and agitated, but kept ambitious and intellectual, by the great democratic ocean which roared below and around it. An immense distinction between rich and poor—a nobility sumptuous, wealthy, cultivated, yet scarcely elegant or refined; a people with mighty aspirations for more perfect liberty, but always liable, in a crisis, to be influenced and subdued by a deep-rooted veneration for the very aristocracy against which they struggled;—a ready opening through all the walls of custom and privilege, for every description of talent and ambition; but so strong and universal a respect for wealth, that the finest spirit grew avaricious . . . How it may end in the modern world, who shall say? But while a nation has already a fair degree of constitutional freedom, I believe no struggle so perilous and awful as that between the aristocratic and the democratic principle. A people against a despot—that contest requires no prophet; but the change from an aristocratic to a democratic commonwealth is indeed the wide, unbounded prospect upon which rest shadows, clouds, and darkness. If it fail—for centuries is the dial hand of Time put back; if it succeed . . . man will have colonised Utopia!'

But, as the danger of political revolution receded, so did the expectation of an early, or dramatic, social change. Society was in fact changing all the time—and of course still greater changes lay ahead. But, for ordinary people in the middle of the century, it was social stability, rather than change, that seemed real and important. The powerful social energies of the period were still controlled by a powerful social discipline.

Writing in 1902 (in *Studies of a Biographer*) Leslie Stephen looked forward to posterity's judgement on Trollope:

'The middle of the 19th Century—our descendants may possibly say—was really a time in which a great intellectual, political, and social revolution was beginning to make itself perceptible. The vast changes now (that is, in the twenty-first century) so familiar to everybody could then have been foretold by any intelligent observer. And yet in this ancient novelist we see the society of the time, the squires and parsons and officials, and the women whom they courted, entirely unconscious of any approaching convulsions; imagining that their little social arrangements were to endure for ever; that their social conventions were the only ones conceivable. . . .'

Leslie Stephen's prophecy has already come partly true. But Trollope's business was novel-writing, not prophecy, and he described the world as he knew it. Some people had anticipated 'convulsions' in the thirties and forties. In the fifties and sixties, although there was still occasional thunder, the storm seemed to have passed.

Not that Trollope was altogether oblivious to social change. He realized that society had to evolve and he was even ready to welcome the evolution, provided it was not hurried. In *Ralph the Heir* he reflected on changes in landed proprietorship:

'. . . the broad-acred squire, with his throng of tenants, is comparatively a modern invention. The country gentleman of two hundred years ago farmed the land he held. As years have rolled on, the strong have swallowed the weak,—one strong man having eaten up half-a-dozen weak men. And so the squire has been made. Then the strong squire becomes a baronet and a lord, till he lords it a little too much, and a Manchester warehouseman buys him out. The strength of the country probably lies in the fact that the change is ever being made, but is never made suddenly.'

George Roden, in *Marion Fay,* looked on the period around 1880 as one of transition between feudalism and social equality; as a radical he would personally have liked to accelerate the change, but he expected it to take centuries.

In one respect Trollope could see that change was already coming—and coming much too fast for his liking. Like Disraeli he was struck by the shift in power from land to finance. In *The Way We Live Now* he satirized the substitution of plutocratic for aristocratic values. 'In a progressive civilisation', says the radical Stephen Morley in Disraeli's *Sybil,* 'wealth is the only means of class distinction. . . .' Trollope was no despiser of wealth; but a society which had no other criterion of rank would not have seemed to him civilized.

No doubt, in their feeling for the landed gentry and for aristocratic statesmen, Trollope's novels underrate the immense contribution made by the industrial and commercial middle class to the political and social, as well as to the economic, life of Victorian England. It is clear that, for most of the nineteenth century, middle-class businessmen were stongly placed to influence political decisions and to impose their outlook on other classes. But, wherever the basic power lay, the aristocracy was still the ostensible ruling class. For all the restrictions on its freedom of political choice, its social prestige was still firmly rooted. Although the 'entrepreneurial ideal' triumphed widely,[1] it never triumphed over the ideal of gentility, if only because there was never a fatal clash between them. Here again, Trollope gave a faithful picture—at least of the part of England that he, and most of his readers, knew best.

The novelists' picture of Victorian England would of course be more complete if they had studied the industrial middle class more closely. (As it is, we have to rely on Mrs. Gaskell's *North and South* and some rather perfunctory sketches by Dickens and Disraeli.) Similarly, for all their sympathy with the poor, the novelists never really gave a thorough description of the labouring class, whether urban or rural. But, in concealing or ignoring some social classes—or in partially and dramatically revealing them— they reflected the experience of their readers. As Thackeray bitterly confessed, in *Waiting at the Station*:

'You and I . . . have had hitherto no community with the poor. We never speak a word to the servant who waits on us for twenty years; we condescend to employ a tradesman, keeping him at a proper distance . . . of his workmen we know nothing, how pitilessly they are ground down, how they live and die, here close by us at the backs of our houses. . . .'

Thackeray was usually less concerned with the distance between rich and poor than with the effect of snobbery on relations between

[1] Cf. *The Origins of Modern English Society, 1780–1880*, by Professor Harold Perkin.

the upper and the middle classes. When he wrote this passage, he had been distressed by the sight of thirty-eight working women about to emigrate to Australia from the Fenchurch Street Station. His heart had been touched by their plainness and modesty, while his acute class sensibility had been exasperated by the thought that, as an educated London man and not a 'hardy colonist', he could not have brought himself to take any of these 'honest, well-recommended young women' home as his wife. He was moved by a sense of guilt to exclaim:

'. . . what I note, what I marvel at, what I acknowledge, what I am ashamed of, what is contrary to Christian morals, manly modesty and honesty, and to the national well-being, is that there should be that immense social distinction between the well-dressed classes (as, if you will permit me, we will call ourselves), and our brethren and sisters in the fustian jackets and pattens.'

Thackeray felt this gulf more keenly, but perhaps made less attempt to cross it, than several of his contemporaries. There *were* Victorians, like Kingsley, who tried to establish a degree of 'community with the poor'. In the country, where ladies visited cottages, the separation of classes was never so total as in the towns. Even in the towns relations between masters and servants were not necessarily unfeeling and impersonal. But there was indeed a very great ignorance, in most middle-class and upper-class homes, of how the poor lived—and often an instinctive reluctance to contemplate an unpleasant topic.

The shafts sunk into human misery by Dickens and other writers disturbed, but also edified, novel-readers. They could console themselves with the hope that something would be done to put particular abuses right—and their own pity seemed already a kind of atonement. If something more than pity was needed, there could be appeals for private charity or pressure for public legislation. Whatever the eloquence of the novelists, most of their well-to-do readers probably assumed that, when misery was acute, this was either due to the improvidence of individuals or to the awful providence of God. It did not suggest to them that the social system needed any drastic overhaul. As a rule, they were a good deal less oppressed than the youthful Thackeray by the 'Gothic society' which had cradled them; they were familiar with it and were content to be dazzled by its 'glittering antique paraphernalia'.

In any case there were justifications at hand. A favourite justification was the way in which the system encouraged useful ambition. The Dean of Brotherton, in Trollope's *Is He Popenjoy?*, frankly delighted that his daughter should become Marchioness of Brotherton, pronounces a *Magnificat/Nunc Dimittis* over her child:

'It is a grand thing to rise in the world. The ambition to do so is the very salt of the earth. It is the parent of all enterprise, and the cause of all improvement. They who know no such ambition are savages and remain savage. As far as I can see, among us Englishmen such ambition is, healthily and happily, almost universal, and on that account we stand high among the citizens of the world. But, owing to false teaching, men are afraid to own aloud a truth which is known to their own hearts. I am not afraid to do so, and I would not have you afraid. I am proud that, by one step after another, I have been able so to place you and so to form you, that you should have been found worthy of rank much higher than my own. And I would have you proud also and equally ambitious for your child. Let him be the Duke of Brotherton. Let him be brought up to be one of England's statesmen, if God shall give him the intellect for the work. Let him be seen with the George and Garter, and be known throughout Europe as one of England's worthiest worthies. Though not born as yet, his career should already be a care to you. And that he may be great, you should rejoice that you yourself are great already.'

The Dean of Brotherton would have applauded Malthus:

'If no man could hope to rise or fear to fall in society; if industry did not bring its own reward, and indolence its punishment; we could not hope to see that animated activity in bettering our own condition which now forms the master-spring of public prosperity.'[1]

The Dean would also have agreed with Adam Smith that men desire 'the consideration and good opinion that wait upon riches',[2]

[1], [2] Both passages quoted in Perkin, op. cit.

rather than wealth itself. So would most ambitious Victorians. It was usually essential to make a fortune first; but real glory was to be got by sitting in Parliament, or founding a landed, and eventually titled, family. In theory, at least, such glory was open to anyone with enough will and ability. Alton Locke believed that there were 'innumerable stories of great Englishmen who have risen from the lowest ranks'. In *My Novel* Lytton maintains that all notions in England 'even of liberty, are mixed up historically, traditionally, socially, with that fine and subtle element of aristocracy which, like the press, is the air we breathe . . .'; but he goes on to emphasize that 'there is nothing which English folks, from the highest to the lowest, in their hearts so respect as a man who has risen from nothing, and owns it frankly'.

Thackeray confirms, in *Waiting at the Station*, that belief in the openness of English life to talent and hard work was very widely held:

'How long ago is it, that our preachers were teaching the poor "to know their station"?, that it was the peculiar boast of Englishmen, that any man, the humblest among us, could, by talent, industry and good luck, hope to take his place in the aristocracy of his country, and that we pointed with pride to Lord This, who was the grandson of a barber; and to Earl That, whose father was an apothecary? What a multitude of most respectable folks pride themselves on these things still! The gulf is not impassable, because one man in a million swims over it, and we hail him for his strength and success.'

One of the most articulate defences of social inequality in a Victorian novel is put into the mouth of Parson Dale, when he preaches his 'political' sermon in Lytton's *My Novel*. The parson's theme is that this life is a preparation for the next and that every condition of men, both rich and poor, has its own peculiar burden to carry. If poverty were not felt as a burden the most valuable energies of the poor would never be aroused; without the desire for improvement there would be no civilization. Inequality forms a nursery for the virtues:

'If there were no penury and no pain, what would become of

fortitude ?—what of patience ?—what of resignation ? If there were no greatness and no wealth, what would become of benevolence, of charity, of the blessed human pity, of temperance in the midst of luxury, of justice in the exercise of power ?'

If there were no rise, no fall,—nothing to hope for, nothing to fear,—'what a moral death you would at once inflict upon all the energies of the soul. . . .'

Mr. Dale preaches that there should be mutual respect and sympathy between rich and poor and that both should so conduct themselves as to deserve it. He concludes with the exhortation:

'If, then, ye would bear the burden of the lowly, O ye great, feel not only *for* them, but *with*! Watch that your pride does not chafe them—your power does not wantonly gall. Your worldly inferior is of the class from which the Apostles were chosen—amidst which the Lord of Creation descended from a throne above the seraphs.'

This exhortation sums up the social gospel of much Victorian fiction, whatever reservations the more radical novelists might have had about the rest of the sermon. Mr. Dale naturally put his case in religious terms (although a humanist could have adapted his arguments). Inequalities of wealth might also have been justified on grounds of economic expediency and necessity, while other forms of inequality could have been defended by belief in the superiority of aristocratic government. But, in an age when religion was powerful and even humanism had a religious temper, the ultimate sanction of social arrangements had to be found in moral principle. This search for moral justification no doubt explains the persistent Victorian tendency to equate social with moral values—to regard the rich as intrinsically respectable, and the well-born as intrinsically distinguished. It also helps to explain the perpetual ambiguity in the terms 'lady' and 'gentleman'.

*　　*　　*

When a given society is credited with a particular social system, the word 'system' tends to suggest a structure that is necessarily firm, homogeneous and all-embracing. In practice, of course, social systems can be loose as well as tight. In many societies—and perhaps in our own today—widely differing views are held on what constitutes social distinction and on how far those who claim it should be envied, imitated or admired. In the loosest form of society, each man would decide for himself whether to acknowledge any social superiors and, if so, whom. He could even select his own social inferiors, provided that he did not expect them to respond.

There is obviously an element of flexibility and uncertainty in any social system. Each individual looks on the world from his own angle. Lunatics construct their own private worlds. Even sane people, living in the same *milieu*, will differ when it comes to the finer shades of social discrimination. When a remote and unfamiliar *milieu* is involved, differences in social interpretation can be great. Distinctions in the upper reaches of society are seldom clear to those in the classes below; nor distinctions in the lower reaches to those in the classes above. In Victorian times, as the novels show, the prevailing social standards were only partially accepted in the industrial towns, while in all classes there were widely different views about the social importance of artists and intellectuals.

Nevertheless the Victorian social structure was, on the whole, a real 'system', both tight and homogeneous. Without too much of a struggle it managed to control, and absorb, its industrial towns and intellectuals. Parliament, landed property and the London season still crowned the social life of the nation. There was an established and consulted order of precedence and a deference towards traditional ways. The outward and visible signs of social importance were too distinct to be mistaken. This homogeneity contrasted with the social complexity of nineteenth-century France after the upheavals caused by the Revolution, the Empire, the Restoration, the July Monarchy and the successive Republics. The differing standards of the old French aristocracy, the Buonapartist nobility and the wealthy *bourgeoisie* provided Proust with nicer opportunities for social discrimination than he could ever have found in England.

Even the conflict between Wealth and Birth was solved by the Victorians in a realistic spirit of compromise. Some worshipped

Birth alone; others worshipped Wealth alone; but most revered them both. There was something vulgar about unalloyed Wealth and something ineffective about unalloyed Birth; the solution was, wherever possible, to combine them. This sense of social solidarity contributed powerfully to the strong national spirit which shewed in the political, economic and intellectual achievements of Victorian England. A looser social system would have been gentler and might have been equally fertile and stimulating; but it could hardly have produced (for good or ill) so concentrated an effort.

Victorian social discipline was tight; but there was too much scope for personal distinction—whether aristocratic or entrepreneurial—for this to result in uniformity. Although the system could be uncomfortable and often painful, it had its compensations: for the unambitious, a sense of security and of 'knowing where they were'; for the ambitious, the interest and the spur of overcoming obstacles and climbing heights. However trivial social distinction might prove on examination to be, the possibility of achieving it, to a greater or lesser extent, gave a sense of purpose to many lives.

Looking back from our own looser society, knit by a common tolerance rather than a common discipline, we may exaggerate both the discomforts and the compensations of the Victorian social system. A comparison between the two economic systems may be relatively easy to make, at least in outline; but a social comparison is more elusive. The Victorian structure still casts such a shadow that it is difficult to see our own society clearly: even when we know what it is not—where it has ceased to be Victorian, we hardly know what it is.

One of the charms of the Victorian social system for the historian is that, although complex, it was also strongly defined. Certain things about it can safely be said, even if they need to be balanced by others. The shape of our own system is more indefinable—and perhaps we are less eager than the Victorians to attempt definitions. Future historians of our social arrangements will at once have too much, and too little, material to study. It may be a relief to them to evoke (without any prospect of experiencing) the splendours and miseries of Thackeray's 'Gothic society'.

Index of Novelists and Their Works

Index of Stations and Occupations

163

THE UNDERWORLD